CORPORATE ETHICS
CONTINUES

D
O
W
N

THE "PORCELAIN CHAIR"

CORPORATE ETHICS CONTINUES

D
O
W
N

THE "PORCELAIN CHAIR"

By; Alan Mermelstein

Have you been mistreated at work, too?

FROM SEX IN THE WORK PLACE,

MANAGEMENT BY INTIMIDATION,

TO DISCHARGE WITHOUT CAUSE!

To order additional copies of this book, contact:
Xlibris Corporation
1-888-795-4274
www.Xlibris.com
Orders@Xlibris.com
52721

Contents

I discuss, the fact that discrimination is still thriving. We should have more wisdom in this modern age of information.

I hope this will help to tie all of the book's contents together.

DEDICATION

I would like to dedicate this book to the following;

To my wife, Mandy for her undying supportive roll and exceptional patience, to my family, particularly David Resnik for his suggestions and constructive criticism, to my helpful friends and finally to Xlibris for their expertise in providing advise and guidance in helping this book become a published reality.

Chapter I

Sharing of some thoughts:
The Double Edge Sword

Employers complain that employees are no longer dedicated and perform like they couldn't care less. However, today's employees question, why should they care or be dedicated, realizing that they have witnessed the **"rewards"** that their **parents** or **grandparents received** after years of dedication. They were the individuals responsible for great contributions, which resulted in providing the catalyst that helped to bring about the great Corporate America's success story.

Their *gift "rewards"* included either a **loss** in **hospitalization benefits, amount of; paycheck, bonus, vacation time**, or it may have bought them a *no charge* scheduled **meeting** with the **chopping block**.

[Tootles and happy job hunting!]

Unfortunately, "there is little reward for dedication, today!"

The ***competent dedicated*** employee is no longer viewed as a company's asset, [probably it's most valuable asset]. It is commonplace for companies to actually consider the associate much the same as they would any other liability.

Unfortunately, payroll is the most flexible overhead that provides a direct effect on the bottom line, allowing most companies to look at it as being a negative.

We all realize that today, companies must continuously evaluate their modes of operation. This requires instituting a great deal of managerial savvy.

We also appreciate the importance of a *legitimate* profit margin. Although, within some industries, the trend seems to be *above* and *beyond* what one might consider as a "normal" profit expectation.

There is a general **lack of concern** as to the effect that some cost cutting measures could produce or **how some lives may be affected**. There is an inherent need to produce a larger over-all increase in the gross profit margin. This will provide more room that will allow for a reduction in the price, as needed to meet or beat competition when using available forms of the advertising media.

We realize that the focus seems to be only on **satisfying** the **Wall Street "players"**. This focus certainly contributes to how, when and in which direction many of the corporate decisions are made.

It is obvious that with most companies, the **focus** certainly is **not** on the **employees, their families' needs, the quality of products** produced, nor is there a great deal of consideration to the kind or level of **customer service** that they *actually* render.

Despite the fact that they give a lot of lip service to the term "**customer service.**"

One would question if there is any significant consideration at all, in regard to Corporate Ethics, by Corporate America.

In this day and age, there seems to be many discussions in regard to *Corporate Ethics,* or shall we say, the extreme lack there of. This is not the first time in history, that a discussion of this topic has been common place along with many other explosive topics.

[We sure do a lot of *talking* about a lot of things, don't we?]

Maybe this time however, complacency and a general acceptance of this less than desirable condition exist in the absence of any protest or a leader to champion the cause.

Could it be that the lack of protest denotes acceptance? Do we really accept the way that the average Corporation operates? **[This is doubtful!]**

One can readily realize how sadly **ethics** and a general care of **fairness** toward others have **disintegrated**. It doesn't require too much time to study or even much fore-thought, anymore then it requires a rocket scientist to recognize these unacceptable conditions.

In general, ethical modes of operation seem to be unapparent by most standards. I am sure that you are aware of this situation, by your every day interactions with "Corporate America."

Do we feel so overwhelmed by the power exhibited from all these great Corporate Giants, that we hear nothing but silence in lieu of any resounding protest?

Is there no leader willing to step up to proclaim that we all have had enough? There is an absolute lack of any **true leadership** in many categories, and the category of leading the way to good *ethical conduct* and *caring for others* is certainly no exception.

While we contemplate this condition, make note that there is also a considerable lack of good role models for our youth of today, to emulate. What a shame that in sports, music, the theater, etc., we seem to be continuously let down. This too is truly a shame but let us continue now, with this book's topic, **Corporate Ethics—**

When one takes into consideration, modern day's extreme numbers of competitors, you realize that it requires a very astute business individual with the ability to plan thoroughly and react quickly. All this is needed, in order to get any market share of the business "pie".

There should be much more consideration or incentive to making good **ethical decisions.** However, this would probably create the feeling that it would interfere with the ability to produce a positive impact on the bottom line.

Have we evolved into a society where absolutely nothing else matters, but the all encompassing >

Bottom line? ~~~~→*Just the bottom line?*

Chapter II

The following are *all true* **case histories** that have taken place over the years. The companies' names have been changed, but I am sure, that without much thought, you will be able to *recognize* quite a few of them. Thus, you can make the connection to their actual names. There is also some *significance* to the names given to the individuals involved, which have been changed to avoid any possibility of being libelous. The names might bring a *smile* to your *face*, but hopefully this will *not diminish* the *seriousness* of the situations that actually took place. Some of these situations, you may have experienced yourself or know of at least one person who did.

In many cases, for the sake of satisfying the bottom line, the people that Corporations choose to place in a managerial position, results in individuals of sheer incompetence. These managers seem to be adhering to unacceptable business practices and/or developing poor business decisions, all leading to actions that this author feels can only be considered as unethical. The lack in ability to properly manage associates, manage business, and/or provide good customer service seems to follow and be commonplace.

Case Histories:

Some of the worst records of questionable ethics can be found in the **Retail Industry**. Therefore, I will start with several examples that will give an indication of the types of situations individuals in retail are confronted with.

RETAIL INDUSTRY:

I. Low Mark's Department Store—A discount dept store.

We start this experience with an Assistant Manager, Hyman Road. Hy Road went to work with the department store as an Assistant Department Manager of Hardware and Sporting Goods Departments. He was soon called into the office and told that he was such a valuable hard working employee that they were giving him the Luggage Dept. to manage, this way they could justify giving him a raise. They did not want to lose the good work ethic of Hy. He remained assistant manager of Sporting Goods and Hardware at the same time. Plus, a luggage department is much like a bastard step child. No one wants to be bothered with it.

After a few months passed, the Store Manager called Hy into the office once again, saying that they felt that he has constantly improved every area he was involved in. The Store Manager said that he was giving Hy another raise and wanted him to take over Sporting Goods. They were splitting the Hardware and Sporting Goods Departments.

Once again as time passed Hy was called into the office. The store Manager explained that they experiencing trouble in the Domestic, Curtains, Drapes, and the Yarn Departments. The manager of those areas had mismanaged causing a serious over stock condition in damaged curtains and drapes.

So, they were going to take Hy Road and send him over to straighten that whole area out.

Unfortunately, they left Desire Moore, the previous Department Manager, in that area, to work under the direction of Hy. You can readily see how this went over like a lead balloon, as far as Desire was concerned. Luckily Hy was used to taking the high road.

Hy started to clean up the department, working hard and trying diligently, to develop an acceptable relationship with Desire. She resented this new young manager, but put on a good front as she falsely acted overly sweet. *[Because she was so pissed off, Hy needed to watch out for the proverbial knife that she likely carried, although well hidden. We all know that she was sure to find a way to get even.]*

After all, she did have 12 years experience managing these departments. Hy Road had enough difficulty trying to pronounce terms like festoon and jabot, let alone know what the hell these terms actually referred to. Despite the fact that Hy went into the area not having the foggiest idea of what a lot of items were, he was a quick study.

When the previous Store Manager was promoted to the Corporate Headquarters in New York City, things started to change for Hy. A new Store Manager was now put in place.

The Buyer from Corporate, responsible for the areas Hy had acquired, seemed to continually by-pass any contact with Hy and continues to address Desire as if she was still his main phone contact. He would even call the store on Hy's days off, to talk with Desire.

One would have expected that the previous Store Manager would have discussed the delicate situation that existed in this area of the store. He should have provided information to the group he worked with at the Corporate Headquarters, including this "Domestics" buyer. What could be the problem? He must know that Desire is no longer the one he should be making contact with.

The new Store Manager had instructed Hy to maintain two mark down records for the over stock curtains and drapes. One was as per the Buyer's authorization and the other was as per the amount of markdown that the new Store Manager instructed Hy to set. The latter was for a larger percent off. One was real and one was for show to keep the Buyer happy as per his authorization, showing a lesser percentage of mark down. Although Hy didn't like this set up, he followed the Store Manager' orders and kept the two records. The falsification of records went against Hy's principals. After all, he was used to taking the high road.

When the Buyer came into town from the corporate office to visit the store, he would take Desire out for at least a 2 hour "lunch". Hy wondered what the hell was going on. Hy was not in need of a meal, but would have appreciated a relationship building secession. I guess that Desire wasn't in need of a meal either. As time went on, Hy realized that the relationship between Desire and the buyer was not just one of a business nature.

[Wake up Hi, this relationship has been staring you right in the face. The only business going on during these so called lunches seemed to be that of "monkey business"].

One day, out of the blue, Hy was called into the office and told that there seemed to be a problem with his relationship in regard to the buyer. *[Duh, you think?]* The relatively new Store Manager said that although there wasn't a problem with his work, the fact that he was unable to develop a good relationship with the buyer, was a major problem.

Consequently, they were going to let Hy go. When Hy asked in shock, when this was to take place, he was told, "I don't think you want to hang around here now, do you?

It sure seemed that Desire wasn't going to take her demotion *lying down,* but apparently would accept the reinstatement of her managerial position, *"lying down". [Whatever]?*

Hy went from hero to heel much like going from 0 to 60 in a relatively New York minute.

It was certainly obvious, that Hy couldn't compete with Desire, at least from a biological stand point.

The buyer seemed to have some other personal *desires,* which he apparently had been able to satisfy with, **[you guessed it]** *Desire.*

Sex in the work place providing job security for this underperforming Manager.

This was done at the expense of a good dedicated employee who had proven over and over, to be a very effective Manager.

Low marks go to Low Marks Department Store.

This was certainly a poor business decision and its now time to ask-

How ethical was that?

II. Arears—A Dept. Store

Years ago, anyone going into retail, was aware that the hours were next to unbearable, the holidays off were non-existing and the pay sucked. [**In plain English**]

The only consolation was that you didn't have any pressure.

Today, retail hours are still bad, holidays off are still non-existing and the pay still sucks, but the extent of pressure is beyond belief. Working retail can be next to unbearable.

Arears went through a real change. They eliminated the quantity of cash wraps, dispensing with the idea of having them in each department and went with centralized cash wraps [retail name for check out]. They were able to cut down to only 1 or 2 cash wraps per floor. They could station four registers within each cash wrap. This way they could call others to help out since there were other registers in waiting.

They use to have well trained associates in each Department. They were capable of supplying the customer with the answers to most all questions they might have.

This proved to be very helpful in providing the customer with the necessary information regarding product location and selection. Customers need to be able to make informed decisions in regard to which product would fit their individual needs, the best.

The company decided to change from providing information that aided the customer. The associate was instructed to just about ignore the customer.

It was ok to recognize, the customer with a "hi or hello" and maybe a "how are you today?" Beyond that, they were to continue stocking merchandise and recovering any areas that were messy.

> *They were instructed that they were only to help the customer, if he or she actually asked you for assistance.*

This allowed them to cut down personal, to a skeleton crew. *[Wow, cutting payroll, this has a positive effect on the bottom line, doesn't it]?*

As far as the customers' questions, they will just have to guess where to look for the items that are on sale and guess which item best fits their needs. *[You're on your own Mr. and Ms. Shopper, lots o' luck! Ignoring the customer is what you will get. This is the latest in Customer service minus.]*

Will the customer be lucky enough to find that one and only associate around, and if they do, will he or she have the time to provide them any assistance at all? Will they even know the answer to any of the questions they may be asked?

In the mean time they set up the cash wraps with cashiers that were told that they had to open new credit card accounts, and sell extended warrantees.

Some of these cashiers originated from other countries were experiencing a very difficult time as it was, trying to converse in English. So much so, that most of the time, the average customer had a very difficult time understanding what the devil they were talking about.

Arears was expecting so much from the people that were the least capable of providing the desired results that Arears expected.

Let me introduce you to Woody Succeed. Woody was recruited from a competitor.

The Store Manager knew Woody very well, because he had worked with Arears in the past and proved to be an excellent Manager. He was hired in the capacity of Assistant Store Manager.

Woody first supervised a storewide housekeeping clean up. This combined with a focus on merchandising projects that needed to be jump started, in order to accommodate the new "modifications," as prescribed by Corporate. This covered two floors in all departments. A lot of major moves were involved.

After about *2 years* the *Store Manager* was sent to another store in Pennsylvania, to address this larger store's big problems.

Arears took an individual with very little merchandising background and promoted him to the position of Store Manager.

This individual, who we will call Mark Destruction, came from a Loss Prevention background. Hello to the Peter's Principal, [which states that an individual will be promoted until he reaches a level of his own incompetence] but I am willing to bet, that they must have gotten him for a low ball salary.

Mark's previous area of expertise was in the control of shrinkage and shoplifting. He didn't know shit from shoe polish, in regard to any merchandising procedure, reading and following a plan-o-gram, or which adjacencies should be developed.

He certainly didn't know the complexities of actually operating a "big box" operation. His display of sheer incompetence was so obviously conspicuous, that even the associates were aware of it.

He was especially behind the eight ball when it came to soft line items. (Men's, Ladies' and Children's clothing, bed, bath, housewares, etc.)

There were many discussions between the Store Manager Mark and the Assistant Manager Woody, regarding merchandise placement.

In one particular case Mark insisted that Woody place fancy Evening Gowns on a rack with casual pant suits. *[Huh, he really said that?]*

This most likely wouldn't make any sense, to most people regardless of their background. The discussion became heated as Woody explained that you just don't associate these two completely different types of clothing together.

Mark Destruction insisted that he was the Store Manager and what he said is what he expected Woody to do, no matter what Corporate or anyone else said.

Mark also demanded that Woody approach the cash wraps every 10 minutes to **harass** the cashiers. He was to ask them how many credit accounts they had opened in the last 10 minutes and how many extended warrantees they sold in the same time frame?

They were the least capable but were gunned to produce the most. The promotion of Mark Destruction proved very destructive. This was the *Peter's Principal* at its finest. Such, incompetence!

Putting a person in a position that is above and beyond the person's *ability*, *training* or *experience* is a poor business decision. Employees and the customers alike suffered the consequences of his incompetence. When we look at this so called Store Manager, we question why was Mark placed in this position, in the first place?

We are forced to also question then, is it ethical to place someone so unqualified, in experience and knowledge in this type of position, where the mishandling of all associates involved, was allowed to take place?

This was done allowing Arears to get him for less remuneration, than they would have had to give to someone who was better qualified.

Later, the Assistant Store Manager, Woody was sent packing when a younger person was willing to work for less ended up replacing him.

He had been constantly told that his salary was more than most others, in a similar position. Arears was looking to merge with another chain and wanted to be as palatable as possible to that end. So there was a total of 655 Managers in similar positions that also lost their jobs throughout the nation, during a two month period. I am sure that this move looked excellent on paper when there were less expensive replacements.

[Hurrah, this is a great move for that ever loving bottom line]!

Shaft the group of managers that had been there for Arears. This way the company could look more palatable for their up coming merger. Any manager making over a certain amount had to go. That included 655 that were *severed* from the Arears *main artery* of managers, as a cost saving measure.

Arears had been experiencing many problems with service and delivery of their appliances, etc. There were many times, when customers would wait throughout the day, despite the fact that they were given a four hour window. They said they were from Arears, but they were an outside delivery service.

Customers could wait for delivery, to no avail. Some customers that had taken off time from work just so they could receive their delivery of merchandise may not have received it that day, after all. There were times when customers were in need of a refrigerator. The drivers would arrive and leave earlier than their scheduled time. This was of course, prior to the customer being able, to get home to receive their delivery.

The customer would then be told that they couldn't get back to them for another two weeks. *[All this time, living with out a refrigerator. Are they really serious? The situation sure is].*

Delivery schedules were made as per Arears' convenience, and certainly not the customers. Allowing the treatment of associates and customers without respect is wrong.

How ethical was that?

III. Dreck's Department Store

Once again this is an example that Retail provides.

We will look at the experience of a Multi-Department Manager. He was called an area supervisor. We will name him Howdy Takeit.

Howdy was managing the Children's Department for the company. Here is yet another case where we have a Manager that had proved himself.

He was called in by the Store Manager who told Howdy that he really needed his expertise in the Men's area.

That amounted to a promotion, which Howdy readily accepted. After a year of successfully managing that area, Howdy was once again brought into a meeting to discuss Howdy's future.

This time however, the Store Manager delivered some bad news. It seems that although the Men's Department was doing very well, the Store, as a whole, was not. The Store had dropped in annual volume, just enough to require this location to drop one Department Manager. The store's present volume could no longer support the same quantity of Department Managers.

They would have to drop one Manager and restructure. This would be accomplished by combining some departments, to make up for the loss of this manager.

Since he didn't have as much seniority as the other Managers, Howdy was the one to be cut. The Store Manager said, "I tried to argue that I preferred to select one of the other managers that has proved to be less effective, to be the one that I cut from this store, but I wasn't successful".

Howdy was then told, that there was an opening in one of the other stores, within the chain. This was a store that was going to close in a couple of years, as it was located in the dyeing Parsely Leaf Mall. Obviously, as the mall goes, so will this Dreck's location.

Howdy had no choice, but to unenthusiastically accept the transfer to their Parsley Leaf Store. There he would manage children's, women's, and the intimate apparel departments.

We will give a name to the tough Store Manager that probably is much kinder than what she deserves. We will call her Phyllis O'Fear. Howdy was soon to find out that most everyone in the store had some very graphic nicknames for her. She had the personality and the temperament to earn all the names she was called, behind her back, of course. They were names like, the "Gestapo Bitch" and "Parsley Nazi", including names that were peppered with too many four letter words to even be worth mentioning.

Phyllis was a terror on wheels. She could only manage by crude, unadulterated intimidation.

> *[When one lacks the ability to be able to effectively manage by motivation, then they usually resort to managing by intimidation.]*

Phyllis loved to page someone and give them just 10 seconds to respond. Not having enough time, would give her a chance to be able to blast their ass. She was a real pro, at chewing them another ass hole. *[She knew how to chew around the circumference which would allow their asshole to just tumble to the floor, so to speak.]*

She purposely wore very hard sole shoes, They took on the appearance of the old "school mom" style of the past. She would stomp her way through all the departments, throughout the store in a way that could strike fear with each thunderous sounding foot step.

She loved to page managers to her office, in a demanding and boisterous voice. She would then *demand* that they to sit down until she was ready for them. Then, she would page another manager and put them on speaker phone. Phyllis then proceeded to ream them out, over the phone, so that the one sitting there would witness the cracking voice, as he or she squirmed, as their shaking hand held the receiver on the other end of the phone.

This was another way of striking fear and keeping control through out the Store.

If an associate was on the phone talking, she would walk over and quickly hit the button to put it on speaker phone. She could then hear whoever was on the other end and most importantly, what they were saying. This was just in case the discussion was about her. *[Guilty conscience, I guess].*

At one period of time when the Furniture Department Manager was on vacation, Phyllis ordered Howdy to take a sofa down to the lower level for a customer and load it on his truck. This was an unusual request.

The problem with this was three fold.

> Number one was that Howdy was almost 60 years old.
> Number two was he didn't have any help.
> Number three there wasn't any support brace available that Howdy could wear for protection.

So, the sofa was lifted with tremendous effort, as it had to be stood on end so it would be able to fit on a small passenger elevator.

[Oh, did I forget to mention that the freight elevator was out or order at the time?]

Howdy ended up with a hernia. His doctor was very emphatic as he warned Howdy, that he was not to lift or move any heavy items anymore.

When Phyllis was told this along with the confirming doctor's note, she went absolutely ballistic. She yelled, "This better not become a compensation case"!

She went to the Children's Dept. and started moving some four way racks, stating "I will have to do this, because Howdy has a hernia, a hernia, he has a hernia" she yelled. She moved the racks with a vengeance. She continuously threw dirty looks at Howdy. She repeated this many times at the top of her lungs so all customers and associates could hear her deep cutting words.

Howdy decided to resign as the continuous intimidation became unbearable. Many Managers and other associates had written to human resources, informing them of the disrespectful way she managed by using her famous intimidation tactics, but to no avail.

Dreck's Department Store allowed this management by intimidation to continue, and continue it still does, even today about six years later.

How ethical was that?

IV. Jose A. Punk Clothiers—Men's Clothing Store

The associate we will meet in this situation will be called Ben Hadd. Ben had semi retired.

He went to work for Jose A. Punk in the shipping / receiving department. He was able to work 25 hours a week while continuing to collect his Social Security.

In addition to shipping and receiving, Ben also would help out on the sales floor. He provided his merchandising expertise, in all the different areas through out the store.

You see, Ben retired from a background of Retail Management, so, it was only natural that he was selected to become the Store Manager, when the existing Manager left.

Ben took over a real challenge. It was a challenge from a merchandising, housekeeping, and most importantly a human resource standpoint.

Sales were also on a downward trend. Ben took on the responsibility, hitting the ground running. During the first six Months, Ben confronted many expected challenges, and in addition there were many that presented a real surprise to Ben.

He inherited only *five* sales people, compared to the *ten* very capable and successful members of the sales staff that existed the previous year.

They also needed to add another part time tailor to replace the one that had recently left due to the birth of a child. A replacement for Ben in the shipping / receiving area was also on the list of needed personnel.

Ben donated many of his days off, which he sacrificed for recruitment purposes. The most monumental challenge was filling the real void in his Management team. Prior to Ben taking over, there was a need for an Assistant Manager, the lack of which added more responsibility for Ben. That was in addition to his already difficult task of turning this store around.

Then there were the many times when a power outage occurred. It happened at least 10 times in a 6 month period, and sometimes as often as twice within one week. Customers had to be escorted out of the store because of the danger that the darkness presented, combined with the inability of having functioning registers. The lack of power continued for periods of up to six hours at a time. This certainly was not good from a business standpoint. There were the many times, that they were unable to approve debits cards, credit cards or catalog orders. [The catalog items too, were paid for at the time of ordering, thus making approval necessary]. This was because of computer problems.

The electrical system malfunction proved devastating for business as did the computer problems.

One day the rooftop air conditioner started leaking down through the ceiling tile. The reason for the leaks was that the A/C system was tilting backwards, due to a problem with the curbing that it had been installed on. Water dampened the dress shirt area under the leak. This rendered some of the shirts worthless.

The curbing had weakened and cracked with age, hence the condensate water flowed backwards and down through the roof.

Then there was the time that the Property owner decided to resurface the parking lot of the whole strip mall. Unfortunately, it started to rain right after the removal of the existing surface. The rain lasted for several days, causing the ground to get super saturated. The fact that the building shaded the parking lot from the sun prevented the unpaved area from drying. It took almost three weeks before they could finish resurfacing and before the lot was once again useable. This certainly put the store in a precarious situation, as they tried to meet and beat last year's numbers. Parking could only be accomplished at a distance away, causing a discouraging long inconvenient walk to the store.

Ben took this all in stride and kept his positive attitude, which he hoped would prove contagious to all the associates.

He presented Power Point sales training to the Sales staff, making sure that there was a heavy enfaces on Customer Service Excellence. So that when the crowds of the customers were ready to come, then Jose A. Punk sales people would be prepared to serve them productively.

Ben continued to use his days off to visit other stores for the main purpose of recruiting. He was putting in many hours, but after all, he was and always had been a "company man".

[Oh what a fool he was, oh yea]!

One Saturday evening, there seemed to be an intermittent problem with the elevator. This store was on the second floor over a video store. Ben instructed the manager in charge that night, to hold off doing anything in regard to the elevator as long as it was working. But, if the elevator stopped altogether, then he should call the elevator people and have them come in on Sunday. Ben was hoping that this wouldn't be necessary as the differential for a Sunday repair was cost prohibitive. However, the elevator was uncooperative and didn't wait for a less expensive time to act up. The elevator stubbornly refused to move at all.

As luck would have it, the elevator stopped on the first floor, Sunday Ben proceeded to open the store and he darted up the steps assuming that the elevator would not operate. He got up the three flights and tried to unlock the door that secured entry to the store. For whatever reason, the stubborn door refused to unlock from that direction. This door usually had been locked and unlocked from the inside of the store.

Ben reversed his direction and hurried down the steps, because he made the decision to take a chance that the elevator might suddenly start up. He was moving as fast as he could go.

He hoped that he wouldn't hear the loud penetrating sound of the alarm going off, which would result in alerting the police and other emergency vehicles to come rushing to the scene, for what would be only a false alarm. This could draw a hefty fee to cover their needless response.

Ben finally approached the last flight, when his right foot quickly slipped behind him on a piece of material that must have fallen out of the pocket of a recently tailored garment.

Ben's body propelled forward, down the remaining six steps, at what seemed to be at rocket speed, continuing head first. The *landing* put up a very hard resistance as it greeted Ben's head, right shoulder, and right leg. This obviously resulted in abruptly stopping his unexpected and forceful descent.

Ben got up dazed and staggered to the elevator, holding his breath, in hopes that he would soon be able to feel upwards movement from that elevator. For a fleeting second he also wondered about the length of time that he laid on the landing or whether the five or six steps he cascaded had resulted in his experiencing an unconscious condition. If he did lose his consciousness, he wondered for what period of time?

Then suddenly, much to Ben's relief, the elevator started to move right up to the second floor store level. He could hear the alarm loud and clear, right through the sealed elevator doors. Then they parted open, providing the path that granted Ben entry into the store.

Ben was able to call the alarm people, explaining his plight in time to ward off the emergence of emergency vehicles.

Ben sat down on his desk chair while getting his bearings. The hectic pace was over now since he had successfully made contact with the alarm people, and he was thankful that he was able to do it in time.

He felt the need to visit the bathroom. It wasn't until washing his hands that he noticed the reflection in the mirror that revealed a huge "egg" protruding from his forehead. It appeared as if he was growing a horn representative of one you would view on a unicorn. Evidently, this was where his head must have "kissed" the floor with a forceful "howdy", upon making impact. This sure does account for his severe headache.

It was awhile, before others would show up for work, because it was company policy that the Manager had to be at work one hour prior to the store opening.

This was of course, to get the store ready for the day's business.

Since the store was shorthanded in regard to Sales People and most importantly an Assistant Manager, Ben decided to fax an accident report to the home office. However, he could not see how he could find the time to schedule a doctor's visit because of this short handed condition. This happened in the month of September.

[Answer the question, was he a company person or just a plain ole' fool? You will soon be able to figure that out for yourself].

December turned out to be a real large month with Super Tuesday beating last year's numbers, [referred to in the retail business as LY numbers].

This showed a doubling of the amount of sales for this same Super Tuesday sale that they were repeating from the previous year.

The economy was on an express slide down, for the first quarter and Ben was struggling to keep things going. However, of all the stores in the Region, this store usually rated at about the half way point in business.

The Regional Manager would state that he didn't want to hear anything about the economic conditions that existed, during his weekly conference calls. The Peter's Principal is showing its ugly head again. He was probably one of the most pronounced examples of it. It's ok to be positive, but let's look at ways to overcome the conditions instead of pretending that they do not exist. Take off the blinders and face facts. Ignoring them doesn't make them go away. *[Hello, are you listening]?*

Ben never received any counseling or had any personal discussions regarding his particular store. He also had absolutely no training as to the company's way of doing things, nor did he receive any orientation manuals. It has always been a fly by the seat of your pants operation. By March, Ben had filled all vacant positions and even had hired and trained an Assistant Manager.

Ben felt that he could now take the time to go to the Doctor. You see, ever since his fall down the steps in September, most all affected areas of Ben's body got better and seemed ok. However, Ben's shoulder kept getting progressively worse.

The results after seeing an Orthopedic Surgeon and having an MRI, proved that he had suffered a torn rotator cuff with three tears. There is no wonder that Ben had been suffering such pain in the shoulder. Surgery was definitely, the name of the game.

Now that Ben was fully staffed, there should be no problem taking off the necessary time for surgery and rehabilitation.

[Isn't that Right? No, sorry but that's W R O N G]!

Ben called the Regional Manager and told him of the results of the MRI and that surgery was in order. This was on a Thursday.

The following Tuesday the Regional Manager showed up, but the message was not good.

The Regional said that since the store was down *[as most other stores were]* he needed to make a change in Store Manager. He slyly suggested that Ben might just want to sell men's clothing in the store, instead of Managing.

Ben reminded him that they were fully staffed, to which the Regional made the statement, "oh well, I was just thinking". Either he wasn't thinking or most likely, this would allow him to say that he had offered Ben a position and that he had turned it down.

[Did Ben's dedication pay off? It certainly didn't for Ben]!

He then told Ben that he wanted him to say, that he left on his own. Ben said, "That is not the way it is coming down". The Regional then responded, "Yea, but this way is less messy".

We all realize that it wasn't the sluggish sales, but that Ben might cost the company money, because he needed surgery and some time off for rehabilitation.

Ben could have returned to work after surgery and handled most of his Managerial duties.

The attorneys tell Ben that the American Family Leave act would apply but, it requires that the company must have 50 employees within a seventy five mile radius. It must include Ben's store, in that radius. Since this was not the case, Ben didn't have a leg to stand on.

Ben was now out of work, with additional bills, and a deflated ego, as a reward for his dedication. Ben really wanted to send Jose A Punk a message that you just cannot continue to treat people like dirt, as a reward for their dedication.

Poor Management on the part of the Regional allowed this injustice to take place. If the Regional was qualified to execute the expected duties that the Regional Manager position normally entails, he would have been there to offer support along the tough road of the seven plus months that Ben was the Manager. He hadn't shown his face very much as Ben Hadd continually provided a can do spirit.

If there had been any real concerns, the Regional would have showed up along the way, and evaluated the management practices of Ben. *(Note; This, of course, did not happened).*

If there was a need of improvement, he could have offered assistance by counseling. That's what someone in his position is supposed to be there for. *[That's his job].*

Provided Ben was doing all that could be expected, than it would be the Regional's duty to let Corporate know, Ben or any store manager, for that matter, is running a tight ship. Conditions beyond their control, is all that is preventing any better sales results. *[**This would be expected, whenever the economy proves to be in deep duty**].*

It is a shame considering all the B.S. that Ben went through for this Company, only to have them spit right in his face. He spent his seven plus months of straightening out the many problems in the name of dedication and providing good managerial expertise. A good Regional would not have allowed this store to get into the mess it was in, prior to Ben taking it over. He would have also recognized Ben's accomplishments. The company is much better off because of Ben, but, is Ben better off because of Josh A Punk?

Once again we see what the unqualified, "so called" Regional Manager's responsibility should be. It is not about golf, fun and games, or operating without the knowledge of how to be supportive to the Store Managers. It takes more than just calling for the "numbers" daily.

He never offered training and orientation for new managers? How helpful was he in recruiting associates, or at least making sure that classified ads were placed. Maybe being supportive is against his beliefs? Did he have the chutzpah to discuss any negatives that may have existed, if in fact any did exist?

Dose he recognize the needs of his Store Managers and prioritize them in a training format? offer suggestions for improvements and give praise when and where appropriate? Today, they place one in a position as if they are just testing the water with their toe. They are ready to pull the plug for any reason, rather than developing Managers for the long haul.

Believe me it is to their benefit that Managers don't fail. If they fail because of the lack of Regional attention, then the biggest failure is the Regional Manager. By the same token, if *any* associate fails because he had not received training or coaching, it is their immediate supervisors fault.

> *[**Come on Managers, get with the program! How many employees did you train or coach today, this week or even this month? If the answer is none than, a huge shame on you]!***

Managers, of all capacities need to accept the fact that there will be times when there may be a need for surgical procedures, or other medical emergencies, and some employees may need time off for

parental needs. There is a life outside of any Company and people do work to live and not live to work! If you do not understand that than you're an unadulterated *FOOL)!*

If you need surgery, than they want you to go away, despite the fact that the Company will not admit that is the reason. You may have been able to perform most of your duties as the Manager after surgery. However, you can't get hired anywhere else, because of your immediate post surgical condition. The Regional doesn't have anything to worry about, as he still has his job and the money to put food on *his* table.

How ethical was that?

V. Mess Seys Dept. Store

This example will show you the types of things that companies are getting away with. Here again we are taking a look at a large, well known chain department store.

We have a Salesman that has been a successful salesman at this store before it was bought out by Mess Seys. He had a fabulous reputation as one of the best footwear Salespeople in that store.

In fact, he certainly could have held his own in a company wide sales competition, if they had one.

There were many times that he received offers from Mess Seys' competitors, in an attempt to recruit him. He stayed with Mess Seys out of dedication.

He had been at this store for fourteen years. You can imagine the shock when they decided to take away one of his three weeks of earned vacation time. This was done by Mess Seys Department Store as a cost saving measure.

It was without recompense, or equivalent time to be used at a future date.

The fact is that he lost one week vacation, which they didn't have any problem providing for his enjoyment, just one year prior. The company policy provided for an earned three weeks off, for the length of service that he had performed. The company just decided not to give the quantity of vacation weeks, that their employee handbook clearly stated he qualified for. He lost that week, like it or lump it.

The next year, he celebrated his 15th year. They said that he had to have continuous employment for 15 years to now receive 4 weeks. The new hand book also said that this was the case. Now that he has 15 years he was excited, expecting what he clearly earned from the Company. However, this time he was told that even though the hand book said that he will get 4 weeks vacation, they have now changed the month that you must have started employment. He will have to wait until his 16th year for the fourth week to start. *[If they don't get rid of him first, I hope he doesn't hold his breath waiting].*

This proves to be quite a savings, when you consider that if they are able to cut an earned vacation week from all qualified associates, they can enjoy quite a savings. Great for the Bottom Line!

Mess Seys sure *messed* up his vacation plans with his family.

How ethical was that?

AN ELECTRONICS RETAILER:

VI. Circle Shittie—Electronics Retailer

This experience will begin with a company that was rolling along in a very successful way. They had experienced very good growth through the United States. Then they made what was to be one of many mistakes.

> *[You know, in the past it really wasn't as big of a problem if a company made a mistake, since, most of the time, they could recover. When you consider today's competitive and economic climate, we are in times that aren't very forgiving, in regard to a company mistake. Some of the largest corporations have experienced being down for the count. While some companies made mistakes that any form of resuscitation was unable to help them to survive.]*

The first mistake was that Circle Shittie made the decision to open a store in their biggest competitor's, (Best Guys) turf. Best Guys returned the favor.

They felt so you want to play, so then get ready to strike the position, because here we come. It didn't take long for Best Guys to set up shop with stores opening up all over the Metropolitan area where Circle Shittie had their headquarters. The outcome was fast and furious, as Best Guys struck a strong competitive blow that proved to be all but a knockout punch to Circle Shittie.

The choke hold delivered by Best Guys' competitive pricing and astute sharp advertising resulted in Circle Shittie's decision to give up selling appliances. They just didn't seem to be able to compete in that area.

Their sales dropped considerably in all departments, across the board. Instead of reviewing their pricing structure, commission set up, control of expenses and their advertising campaign, they mistakenly decided to let their Salespeople go.

Most of their Salespeople were very knowledgeable and were very capable of providing some of the best possible Customer Service. They could answer your questions, and most importantly they could sell.

So, the Circle Shittie's great minds made the dumb decision to let them go as a cost saving measure. "This was the absolute wrong move!" This should have been the last thing they could have ever considered.

They needed more sales, right? So, why would anyone cut out the professionals that made those needed sales happen? This sure displayed an unbelievable lack of understanding that resulted in propelling the Circle Shittie Company in a downward monetary spiral. We all realize that absolutely, nothing happens until a sale is made. Yet, this is the action of the all important brain yaks, that work at the Circle Shittie Corporate office, came up with.

[Take another coffee break and come up with a good idea this time]!

These Salespeople that are now out of work, due to this major layoff, were pounding the streets earnestly looking for any kind of work. Some of their Salespeople were making in excess of $50,000 per year. With such an amount of commissions being earned, certainly proved the definite worth of these salespeople.

If they are making money, than the company is selling more and should be making money, provided that they have a sound pricing structure and a handle on their overhead expenses.

Listen up, Circle Shittie; if you were able to bring the customers in the store, then you could be assured that these people would have been able to sell them.

But instead, some of these professionals were forced into taking jobs paying as little as just $7.00 per hour. This was because there weren't very many real good paying positions open that were in need of Salespeople at that particular time. *[Hurray for you, sitting in your ivory towers at Corporate, cutting the people that make it happen, while protecting your own donkey].*

I wonder how long it will be before you will succeed in the demise of your company, and then you too, will be the ones who will be pounding the streets looking for employment.

[Is it time to give the Executives another raise]?

You got rid of them while protecting your employment. Look in the mirror and put on your thinking cap. You need sales, so getting rid of the ones that make those sales is nothing less then a poor business decision. Not giving a dam regarding what effect this move would have on those employees is morally wrong.

How can you make such a detrimental move with these salespeople and feel that, as long as you are ok, the hell with them?

How ethical was that?

VII. Dullwords Department Store

The manner in which this particular store operated is one that covers a multiple sins. This company has their Department Managers perform a mark out of stock on damaged goods. This usually is a normal procedure but let us take a closer look at the way this practice is executed at Dullwords.

The Store Manager would send out an email in reference to the dollar amount of damages that each department was to mark out of stock. This was done on a regular weekly basis. The Store Manager (Ida Manager) is without any knowledge of what actual departmental damages existed or if there even were any damages at all.

She tells the Department Managers that they must decide which items he or she will "claim" to be damaged even though these items are in perfectly good condition. After marking them out of stock, they will then locate those items on the computer, under that department's inventory.

The list of the "so called" damaged items, were then added back in inventory. This will allow the inventory to remain quantitatively correct, despite the fact that the items were marked out of stock as a loss.

The *total* dollar value of these falsely stated damaged items marked out of stock, ranged from $1500.00 to $3000.00 per week per department.

Obviously, the end result is that Dullwords could now report to the Government that they did not earn as much as one might think, because of their supposed loss due to (false) damages.

However, the so called "damages" were left on the sales floor to be sold at regular price. **[Remember there wasn't anything wrong with this merchandise].**

When adding up the total of weekly damage dollars, collectively from all departments within the Store, will give you a view of the magnitude of the mind boggling amount for this store alone. One would wonder if they actually follow-thru with this practice throughout the whole chain and not just Manager Ida's store of which we write.

This practice really isn't surprising when viewing the morals displayed, as indicated in the following examples.

We are really looking at one huge amount of money that has a very significant impact on what this company reports to Uncle Sam. This will surely augment their ***Bottom Line***.

Dullwords has a policy that tracks the associates' sales *per hour* (sph) goals. If the associates don't maintain sales as per their goal, they could loose a dollar amount off their hourly paycheck.

After missing the goal a few times, they could even lose their job.

It does not make any difference how well they work, how punctual they are, the fact that they have a good attitude, or whether the store is busy enough to support their individual goal. I know that goals need to be attainable. However, I understand that these goals were developed by taking an average of all the stores in the chain. Then dividing the resulting decision of that individual store's goal, by the amount of sales associates which resulted in what they are calling the associate's goal.

Since this has no direct relationship on what this particular store or associate is capable of selling, proves this to be a very unfair and inaccurate way of determining an individual's goal.

Let me introduce an associate who we will call Emma Victim. Emma had worked for Dullwords for 5 years part time. She had not ever called out sick nor was she ever late. Best yet, unlike most sales associates she always made her sph goal, partly helped by the hours that she worked.

One afternoon while she was helping a customer, she noticed another customer with a bag. Emma readily realized that this customer had a return and she also estimated that she would be involved for awhile taking care of her present customer. Emma suggested that the customer take her return to the nearby register, since Emma would be awhile with her present customer.

The customer thanked her and went to the other register where there were no other customers present, at this time.

Without even attempting to take care of this customer that had the return, the other sales associate quickly approached Emma at almost a running speed. Her speedy approach was silent until she hauled off and slugged Emma with all the force she could muster, right in the upper arm. She evidently didn't want to handle another customer because it soon would be her time to go home.

The next day Emma Victim went to the now new Store Manager and discussed in detail the situation that took place the day prior. Later that day, the Store Manager called Emma into his office and told her that he was letting her go, because of the incident. He also let the other sales associate go. [*It is very surprising that the victim in this case was also punished*]. This happened even though the customer that Emma Victim had been helping witnessed the attack. That customer provided, in his own hand writing, documentation showing an accounting of events that took place that supported Emma's side of the story. She still suffered the consequences of being a victim.

This new Store Manager on another day and time made some sexual advances toward a female Department Manager. This happened behind the closed doors of his office. The fact that she turned down his advances behind closed doors, probably was the reason that this very good Department Manager lost her Job.

Her case ended in court where she was successful in winning a law suit in a sexual harassment case. I guess this is the time to look at all these known indiscretions and ask,

How ethical was that?

Let us look at a few in the food industry:

VIII. Downer Meat Company—

This is a meat processing plant. We will meet a "beef boner" that worked for them, part time. A beef boner is one who takes a hind or forequarter of beef and cuts the beef off the bones. When he gets finished, he will have the bones in one area and meat in another. He has actually "deboned" the beef.

The next step would be to cut this beef into steaks, roast, stewing beef, and even grind it into the ever popular chopped beef (hamburger,) etc.

This beef boner we will call Ben Hurt. There were the many times that Ben was called to this part time job without much notice. He worked full time for a competitor meat packing plant.

Most of the time when Ben would receive a call, that he was needed to work at Downer. This happened when they had a condition that required immediate attention.

You see, when a steer would *die* in its pasture, this company would hook a chain around its hind leg and then it would be dragged in to the slaughter house for quick processing. These animals, diseased as they may be, should have been disposed of not ever processed. They are referred to as "downers".

Because of the fact that there was only an occasional "downer" the owner had stated many times that a little bit of poison in a large sea will not hurt anybody. *[Yea right, tell that to the meat inspector who will never get to see what is really going on here]!*

One day Ben went into work only to find the meat that he was to work on that night was partially frozen, due to the previously described situation. The condition of this type of meat is sticky at times hence it is then frozen to prevent it from deteriorating any more. The owner had forgotten to take it out of the freezer in time at the Downer Meat Company.

Timely processing was of the essence, before the inspector came. That is why this beef was being "processed" at night.

The preceding information explains why an accident happened to Ben.

The catastrophic effect of the frozen beef was that Ben found his knife would slip now and then, as he hit frozen spots on the beef while he tried to work. That is when the unexpected event took place. The knife not only slipped, but was abruptly stopped at its final resting spot, Ben's non resistant left eye. It actually penetrated Ben's eye stopping only after it penetrated right through the cornea.

Ben was barely able to navigate his way home. His handkerchief covered his left eye which only presented blurred vision at best.

The once neatly folded white handkerchief was now saturated with the liquid humor from his newly injured eye.

He was greeted at the door by his shocked and concerned wife and son who promptly rushed him to the hospital's emergency room.

After surgery and 1 year and many months of treatment, Ben had his eye sight finally restored to an acceptable 40/20.

Ben found that the Downer Meat Company just couldn't care less about the unfortunate injury that happened to him almost two years ago. The important thing to remember is that the company was negligent by not giving the meat the necessary time to properly thaw. Plus, the Downer Meat Company was illegally providing diseased food for human consumption, and some how they maintained a clear conscience about the whole escapade.

Ben received absolutely no recompense, and didn't even see a representative from the company. There wasn't even a phone call to see how he was doing. They just distanced themselves from Ben, as if he had the plague and they were afraid of catching it. They didn't even return his phone calls. He could be a liability to them now. Ben unfortunately, let them get away with it. The company is now out of business, but I really wonder how many other companies are operating in a similar manor, to this day?

How ethical was that?

A SUPERMARKET CHAIN:

IX. The Areas Private Market Co.—a grocery chain business

This story starts when a well respected employee who I will call Harry Situation, received a phone call. It was the District Manager; Dave who stated, that he wanted him to go to one of the chain's other locations.

He was to check out what was actually going on there, as there had been some questionable rumors. The market chain was going to use this Department Manager as a trouble shooter from this point on. That was the message that Dave made perfectly clear during this phone call.

The problem that Harry was to check out seemed to be in one particular area. It included dairy, frozen foods and the deli.

There was one Department Manager in charge of this area. Harry was to check out the rumors, thus separating fact from fiction.

Harry Situation proceeded to that store's location, despite the fact that he had no idea what he was actually looking for.

Harry spent only one week, but it actually seemed as if he was there for a month of Sundays. Harry actually received not only an eyeful, but also an earful, which started from day one.

Harry told them at the store, just as he had been instructed that he was there to help them out. "The District Manager Dave sent me," he quickly explained. "I will provide you with an extra pair of hands". *[And eyes and ears, which he purposely didn't mention.]*

Now, let me warn you that although this happened a few years ago, what you are about to read you may find upsetting, and that it may even sicken you.

You may even find these happenings hard to believe.

Harry first viewed the Dept. Manager Simon Nella, in the back room with his crew. They were throwing knives at a target that they had predominately posted on the wall within close proximity to the phone. Yes, it was target practice time. This was, of course a safety hazard as well as a waste of Company time. *[Where, oh where is the Store Manager]?*

However, this was really a minor event compared to what Harry was to eventually experience.

Later that day when Harry was going into the walk-in freezer, to his surprise, he found Simon standing right there as he opened the door. He certainly was not alone. As Harry continued on to get some frozen dinners for the frozen cases out on the floor, he walked past Simon. He was with one of the cashiers in the freezer where he had been, with the door closed before Ben had entered. This could be referred to as a *close* encounter of an *intimate* kind.

She was extremely attractive and built like a brick shit house, you know what I mean, and Simon apparently was in a *position* to know better then anyone. Simon had the cashier's top pulled up and they were in a no holds bared embrace. Simon seemed to be trying to keep his hands warm by snuggling them under her halfway pulled up sweater. Simon and the cashier continued what they were doing and paid no mind to Harry's presence, as if he was the invisible man. *[They were obviously taking care of business, sexual business].*

Harry couldn't avoid providing a parting comment to the cashier as he was leaving the freezer, "aren't you cold" he asked. (Note: the freezer would get down below 22 degrees Fahrenheit over night.)

Her reply was deliberate and void of much fore-thought, "I am never cold when I am with Simon Nella," she bellowed out.

The next day, Harry witnessed one of the most disgusting things that he had ever seen. Harry was to find out that the nonsense would get started right from the beginning of each day.

Simon was preparing chickens to be barbecued. He thought it was a funny, though a crude display, he dropped his pants and with him fully exposed, he portrayed a disgusting sexual act with one of the chickens, prior to placing it on the skewer.

He than placed it in the rotisserie after applying Bar-B-Q sauce.

> *[This chicken will soon be ready for family consumption, "sickening."]*

Simon's disgusting acts didn't end there. A customer asked to get some fresh potato salad from the cooler in the back, as the one in the deli case looked dried out. You have to stir the salad frequently or the cool air in the case will dry it out. Obviously this procedure had not been followed.

Simon was upset with this request that seemed to interrupt him from continuing *whatever* he was doing at the time.

When he went into the back to dish out 2lbs of the requested salad for this real nice lady, he made sure that he spit in the container, while he stated that she will probably think that this was the best salad she ever tasted.

The laughing could have been heard outside of the back room, where Simon was enjoying the fact that he was the center of attention while entertaining the other associates.

Too bad the customer had no idea what was really going on.

All the associates joined in the laughter which was loud and accompanied by one individual actually applauding with chants of that should fix her ass!

There were enough events witnessed, that could fill a book, in just the short week and that was why Harry was trouble shooting this store.

Simon was even seen with pepperoni down his pants, just for laughs. I think that you have the idea with just these few disgusting examples as to the kind of things that were taking place at this store. These were a few examples and believe me there were a lot worst acts that actually happened above and beyond anyone's imagination.

Then came the meeting at the District Manager's office which included the District Manager Dave and Harry, who was struggling to find the words that would describe the disgusting accounting of what he witnessed. *[Now are you ready for the surprising response?]*

Dave stated that despite the fact that this was very upsetting, Simon Nella is a real "bull" at packing out stock. He can put out more work than most other people. We will have to ignore his actions because we would have to add more people to our payroll, if we have to replace him.

Despite the crude and unhealthy actions of Simon, the Company was willing to look the other way in order to save payroll dollars.

They could not take action, since that action had the potential of negatively affecting the ***bottom line***, by increasing payroll.

How ethical was that?

THE PHARMACEUTICAL INDUSTRY:

X. Runt Pharmaceutical Company

This was a Small Company in Small Town America.

Once again this company had a General Manager that was less than qualified. He displayed a degree in Animal Husbandry, however he knew very little about the Pharmaceutical Industry. I will call him Mack Deknife.

Let me introduce a Salesman with the Company that I will call Hugh Gettit. Hugh had been working extremely hard detailing Doctors and calling on Drug Stores, so that he could Introduce Runt Pharmaceutical Company's specialty items. He was doing a great deal of traveling and working somewhere in the eastern part of upstate New York.

The Company was unique as it was not only owned by Doctors, but the board of directors also consisted of Doctors. Note: later it became illegal to have this type of arrangement, as it was clearly a conflict of interest.

The Doctors would most likely write prescriptions for their company's products, regardless of which product would be best suited for their patient's condition. As always, there was a way around this situation, like with most regulations.

All they had to do was put their Wives' names down as the owners of the company. So, this blip in the road was easily resolved.

Now back to Hugh Gettit. He was calling on a Commissioner of one of up state New York's Counties. Hugh had spent enough time with this particular Commissioner, building a rapport so that he knew the initial orders for his company's generics drugs were inevitable. Hugh was moving the Company's exposure further north and south to prospects that knew little to nothing about Runt Pharmaceuticals.

Probably, the most really magnificent display of Hugh's resourcefulness and tenacity was demonstrated by the way he had reacted, after he read about a new serious problem that developed at a well known local Race Horse track. The Race Horses were coming down with the flu. The horses were displaying all the most commonly known flu type symptoms. For many it was just too late to do anything to save them.

Those that did survive ended up with a *cough* and a *lingering* stiffness, which really is the last thing anyone would want to see in a Race Horse.

Hugh spent many nights at his Company office, burning the midnight oil. He spent hour after hour studying reference books like the PDR (Physicians Desk Reference). He researched so; he could be able to determine whether there might be products that he would recommend. Which of the products that his Company sold, that might prove helpful.

He knew that he had done his "home work" and that he had done it well, so he packed his car with samples and headed for the track.

He asked around and found out where he could find the track Veterinarian. He met with Doctor Harold and provided him with gallons of his Company's private label Cough Syrup, an Arthritic Injectable and some other Items that seemed appropriate.

He explained that he was leaving them with the good Doctor to try. He hoped that he could evaluate them to see what help, if any they were able to provide.

Time passed and after a few weeks, Hugh was ready, once again to hit the road so he could keep the appointment that he had made the day prior with Doctor Harold. The Doctor met with Hugh in his office and was quick to cut to the chase. He stated that although not one product alone was a cure-all that the combination of all the products really did provide much needed results.

When Hugh asked if the Doctor would consider putting his findings in writing, the Doctor answered "no, but if your company presents it in writing to me, provided that I agree with what is stated, I will gladly sign it".

Hugh went back to the Company only to find that he was offered absolutely no assistance in writing what could be a monumental promotional piece. "We have to get this into the Veterinarian trade magazines", Hugh thought. So Hugh spent days writing what he hoped would be a great promotional article that would help to sell Runt's products, while it avoided exaggerations or falsehoods.

Hugh went back to Doctor Harold and left the write-up with him to peruse at his leisure, hoping he would decide to endorse it with his most respected signature.

It wasn't long after that day that Hugh was told that he was not *to go back* to the *Doctor* at the track. They were hiring a woman, Helena Cazena, who would now handle that area. She also would handle business in the county where Hugh had worked so hard to develop the great rapport with that County's Commissioner.

It wasn't too much later in time that Hugh found out that the Doctors, who in actuality owned Runt Pharmaceutical Co. had reasons for removing Hugh from those areas. Those decisions were made because they were running this entity at a loss.

The loss that Runt Pharmaceuticals had been experiencing was helping them with their taxes and because of those negative numbers, had been working very well for them.

Since Hugh came to the company without a Pharmaceutical Sales background, there was absolutely no reason for the Doctors to think that someone without this industries experience could possibly screw up their well planned set up. But he did by actually bringing on an appreciable amount of business. Hugh actually thought, that he was supposed to be contributing earnestly to the *success* of this company. *["Shame on him, how could he want to promote this company's business]?* Hugh had already been disappointed in what he had experienced in the Doctors' past actions. He once witnessed one doctor at an office meeting, with his foot on an open desk drawer while he frequently spit on the floor. Not what you would expect from the little "Gods" that they presented themselves to be. This proved to present just another disappointment.

Now, let us discuss the General Manager. It was late one evening after all others had left for the day, that General Manager, Mack Deknife sat in discussion with Hugh. He said, "Now Hugh, I have something very confidential to discuss with you. I have a plan that will make you and me very rich. You will have to be very careful and not mention this to anyone. I can get my hands on amphetamines and I will see if I can have them stored at our Office Manager, Marylou's house. She too, will have to be very quiet about this, and not let anyone know. Mums the word, got it?

All *you* will have to do is make contact with the different truck stops and the drivers of the eighteen wheelers will buy them, to stay awake, of course. We can supply the rest stops on the New York Thruway as well as all the other places. So, are you in?" Hugh felt pressured but was very quick to make his feelings known.

Hugh said, "The fact that this is a hush, hush project and that you want to make arrangements to store the product at someone's house, outside of the business, is a strong indication that this is an area that I should not agree to get involved in".

Despite the reality that this plan never took place, Hugh never forgot what Mack had asked of him, nor did Mack forget or forgive Hugh for his negative response. Mack felt that Hugh really screwed up a good chance that Hugh could have made him a lot of money. There wasn't any discussion that this could mean jail time if they were caught. You can rest assured that it would have been Hugh that would have had his freedom restricted by prison bars. Mack would have denied any knowledge of this plot, while he enjoyed the remuneration that it had provided.

One day Mack asked Hugh to go with him to Glens Falls, New York. He said that he had made arrangements with a person that didn't have professional contacts, but had many social contacts. He stated that "she could hook them up with a lot of her friends in the area, that would buy our over the counter items. "Why she knows everybody up there" Mack remarked.

"Now that you have our headache remedy and cough syrup in the local drug stores, we will make sure that someone actually buys them". Mack asked Hugh to drive them there in his own car, so that while Mack met with this so called "influential" person, Hugh could call on some accounts in the area.

When they got there, Hugh was shocked to see that they were going to a residential location to be greeted by this very attractive sexy woman, who was the owner of this very modest home. Hugh was introduced to her and than he got back into the car to go about detailing Doctors.

When he returned he was directed into the house where the woman, who I will call Evelyn offered Hugh a drink. You could easily see that there had been a lot of drinking going on, since the time that Hugh had left. It was obvious that they had not *indulged* in soft drinks, by any means. This was evident because of the alcoholic odor and the manor in which both of them conducted themselves. Hugh was wondering if that was all that they had *indulged* in.

There were several trips like this and Hugh became sure that there was a lot more to the reason for these trips than Mack was indicating. The assumption was confirmed on one of the return trips from Evelyn's house. By now Hugh had met Evelyn's husband Tony, who would usually come home as Mack and

Hugh were about to leave. It was on one of the return trips back home that Mack opened up.

Mack proceeded to admit that he and Evelyn went back many years. "You see, he told Hugh, my wife is going through the change and I visit Evelyn once and a while to have my *needs* addressed." On one of the trips, Hugh finished his work and returned to Evelyn's house a little earlier than expected.

As he got there, and pulled into the driveway, he saw Mack across the front seat of Evelyn's Car. Upon closer inspection Hugh realized that Mack was on top of Evelyn and slapping her with both sides of his hands. His arms were swinging so wildly that it appeared that he was trying to shake his hands free of his arms, the way tree branches would wave off their leaves on a very windy day.

Wow, this was not only unexpected, but of course unacceptable. Hugh could not just standby and watch this. Despite the fact that there was at least a one hundred pound difference in Mack's favor, Hugh pulled Mack off of her using all of the strength that he could muster. They got into a fight in the back yard, where Mack could be heard yelling that he was going to knock Hugh's damn shit-n head clear off his f—ing shoulders.

Mack came close to accomplishing this task. He sure did beat the crap out of Hugh. After all, it wasn't an even a contest by any means.

Now, are you ready for this? When the violence ended, the two opponents had to take a sixty mile trip back home, in the same car. You could hear a pin drop between this General Manager and his Salesman "chauffeur", who was feeling every bit like a limp dish rag, but with the added element of pain.

Evelyn had three kids and the fact that she and her husband Tony were Italian, sure contributed to the fact that they both had jet black hair. So did two of the three kids.

The youngest boy was a blond, coincidentally much like Mack and even had some of the same feature characteristics, which really seemed very suspicious. Hugh sure felt that Mack had something to do with that, but of course, kept his mouth shut.

One day Hugh received a call from Evelyn and she told him that she appreciated the way he came to her defense. She admitted that her youngest was in fact Mack's. She had been drunk when it happened and Mack held it over her head for years, saying that he was going to tell her husband if she didn't continue satisfying *his* needs. She said that she was afraid to break it off in the past. She finally got the courage to admit to her husband about her past transgressions.

She explained to him, that the reason the recent event with Mack took place was because she had refused Mack. That he then blew his top. She ran out of the house and jumped into her car, where she was trying to get away. Mack caught up with her before she could get the car started. Hence, the slug fest that Hugh had unexpectedly been involved in with Mack.

Hugh was shocked to find out from the Office Manager Marylou that she had been ordered to stroke checks *[write and sign]* on a regular bases for Mack, prior to the trips to "visit" Evelyn. She said that the family room of Evelyn and Tony had been paneled courtesy of Company money. Evelyn had called Runt Pharmaceutical to express her gratitude for the money and adding that the paneling looked great. She had spoken with Marylou who found it extremely easy to add one and one and come to the obvious conclusion.

You didn't have to be a mathematician to realize that they sure added up to two.

Mack was never told of the phone call, but Marylou now knew where his "expense" checks had been going. Obviously, at least one check was for paneling. Hugh couldn't figure out why Tony hadn't realized the obvious in regards to his youngest boy, and how was that family room paneled without Tony questioning where the money came from. They were not rich people by any means. Didn't he know or didn't he want to know?

Hugh could not stand to see any *man take advantage of a woman*. That was true even if the man was his boss. This situation was once again about to become evident.

Despite the fact that the relationship was already extremely strained between Mack and Hugh, the upcoming event was by all means, the last straw.

One evening shortly after Marylou, the Business Manager arrived home to her apartment; she proceeded with the chore of ironing some clothes. She had already set the ironing board up and started to iron in her living room. A knock suddenly came at her door and she could easily see through the peep hole that it was Mack standing there. He exclaimed in a fairly boisterous voice, "Marylou I brought something that I really need your signature on". She let him into her apartment, never expecting that he could be any type of a threat to her.

Once he entered her home, she returned to the task of Ironing. He then appeared to start removing some papers out of a file folder that he had conspicuously tucked under his right arm when he entered. Then to Marylou's surprise, he suddenly lunged at her, holding her tightly by the arms while trying to force kiss her.

He must have thought that she would be a good replacement for the now ended relationship he once enjoyed with Evelyn. But he picked on the wrong one. Marylou was very thin, but strong for her size while being packed full of determination. She warned him to get away several times, but to no avail. Finally, she reached over and lifted the iron. She then let ole' Mack have it right across his right cheek.

> *[He sure was going to have some explaining to do in regard to this red first degree burn that conspicuously replicated the shape of an Iron.]*

He ran out of the apartment holding that clearly visible burn mark on his face. He left so fast that the bogus file and its contents still laid scattered on the apartment floor.

Marylou was fired the next day and Hugh quit as soon as he found out what had happened to Marylou.

Once again the Peter's principal came into play as Runt Pharmaceutical allowed Mack to continue on without the company providing any needed supervision.

The Runt Doctors tried to keep their business running for the write-off that it provided, but finally they were forced to close their doors by the FDA.

They had been willing to hire a General Manager and Salespeople who were unqualified. They thought for sure that this would help them to operate at a loss.

No concern was shown for how things were run as long as the end results would be that the Doctors would be able to line their pockets with the tax money that they didn't have to pay, while this entity was set up to be operated at a loss.

How ethical was that?

CIGARETTE MANUFACTURING INDUSTRY:

XI. Cancer Stick and Emphysema Inc.—Cigarette Manufacturer.

This Company had many sales people on the road calling on Drug Stores, Grocery Stores, Tobacco Distributors and any other businesses that sold cigarettes. Cigarettes were good items to carry, as most of the time the profit derived from them would at least pay for the business's electric bill and sometimes a lot more.

This Cancer Stick and Emphysema Inc. Company had a District Manager who I will call Cary Hon. Cary would hold meetings every morning somewhere in his district. The meetings were held at a location of *his* convenience. This was usually dependent on the territory of the salesperson that he was working with that day.

Yes that's it, all the sales people had to drive to wherever he was located, for a so called "meeting". The meeting was always in the territory of the unfortunate Salesperson that Cary was going to work with that day. The word meeting in this case was a definite misnomer. It was more like a one way yelling session.

He expected each and everyone to jump thru hoops at his command. Cary would demand more sales calls then the company had established as a goal. If you didn't reach the almost unattainable goal, you would meet with the ranting rage of Cary Hon.

He could be seen hiding and spying on his people, behind trees or sitting in his parked car at times, to make sure that the Salespeople were actually working.

The worst part of being involved with Cary was another excellent example of the "Peters Principal" combined with a heavy dose of disrespect for anyone and everyone.

He stated many times that he was going to make it to the top of the Company, no matter how or who he had to step on to accomplish that. It was extremely embarrassing to travel with him to accounts.

The sales person who I will call, Les Reward dreaded to see Cary Hon ride with him because of the fact that Cary's actions were so terribly embarrassing.

Stores carried cartons of cigarettes displayed on shelves. Most companies pay for shelf space. Those that are at eye level will cost more than the bottom shelves. This is a way for the cigarette manufacturing Company to assure that they have the best location and the right amount of space to promote their product, which was in this case, cigarettes.

While in one of the stores of Les's customer, it was Cary that noticed a carton of a competitor's brand of cigarettes that was sitting on their shelf. Cary Hon demanded that one of the cashiers get the Store Manager and get him right now!

When the Manager came out to see what the problem was, Cary proceeded to yell and really read him the riot act. The Manager said that, "most likely someone set that one carton on Cary's shelf by mistake" and he was very sorry that Cary was so upset.

He further told Cary that, he had just come back to work after having heart surgery and couldn't afford to get upset, himself. To this Cary Hon said, "I really don't care if you f—ing die. It's your job to keep this straight; you are supposed to be the Manager"!

Shortly after this incident, Les quit the company. This was the worst display that Les had been exposed to with Cary. Cary always had a bad attitude and a vulgar mouth, but this incident was just too embarrassing for Les to put up with. It was time to move on.

Cancer Stick Emphysema Inc. kept Cary Hon for several years even though many decent Sales People left the company, who had been under his **direction**. *[Do you think we should call it duress instead direction]?*

Many salespeople had sent their letter of resignation directly to Corporate Headquarters and explained the conditions that they were working under. They actually circumvented their so called District Manager, which should have sent a strong message to Corporate in regard to their *MR. CARY HON*, who sure knew how to carry on. It just didn't seem to matter as far as Corporate was concerned.

How ethical is that?

XII. Shaftem Good Inc.

A Rent and own, home furnishings company

I once had the unfortunate opportunity of spending a day riding with a salesman as he drove from home to home collecting regular rental payments from customers, while selling them additional items. The customer would make a certain quantity of rental payments, which eventually would convert to the customer having ownership of the item(s).

We will call him, the salesperson / collector, Sam Theman. He had a very nice personality and a lot of his customers really looked forward to his visits, weekly, monthly or by-monthly as per agreement.

We finished his first stop that morning. He smiled (as we left her modest abode) and stated that he would have stayed longer with this very attractive woman, if I wasn't along for the *ride*. He joked that if he was able to stay longer with her, he would be the one that was *riding*, and he added, "If you know what I mean?" He stated that she was damn good in bed, or wherever they were, at the time.

Then he shocked me when he said that this woman's account had been paid up for two years and as long as she doesn't say anything, Shaft Them Good wasn't going to either.

"The company expects us to be a *good company person, if you know what I mean*". He dragged the words out in what sounded almost like a southern drawl.

> *[He had been collecting from this woman for two years of which she owed absolutely nothing, and then having his way with her to boot].*

He said that "once in a while I tell 'em that I will pay this months payment for them, since they provided services rendered. They think that I'm really doing them a favor," and once again he exclaimed, *"If you know what I mean."*

> *[This was followed with a sickening dirty chuckle].*

This company actually encouraged that their salespeople were to continue collecting, even though the customer was paid up. The sexual favors may have been Sam Theman's doing, to prove that he is "the man," and for his pleasure.

The Shaftem Goode Company actually provided him with paper documentation for additional false rental payments. They would claim that the additional payments were required for Sam's use so he could continue to collect even though the rental had been paid off.

If a customer were to ask when she will be finally paid up, the answer was always that, in two payments they will have paid off their late charge. This would give Shaft Them Good, two more weeks to really push one or more additional items.

That would allow the customer to maintain the same amount of payment that the customer already had become accustomed to paying. They would get something new and Sam could continue to *milk* them *dry*.

How ethical was that?

LET US LOOK AT THE INSURANCE INDUSTRY:

XIII. Mutual Of Oh-My-Heart Insurance Co.

This is a company that really did go too far. We find a newly State licensed Insurance Agent joining the Mutual Of Oh-My-Heart Insurance Company, the Ripoff Agency. Let's call the Agent, Adam Fool and we enter this experience as Adam goes out with his Manager who we will call Phil O'lies. They proceed to an older woman's house, who had called for an explanation of her benefits. She was looking forward to retiring.

Her house is very modest and in very serious need of repair. Adam wondered if the need of such extensive repair was even possible. Could it be worth it, when a place is in such poor condition?

Phil had sold the policy to her many years ago. He was here now; she hoped to provide her with some good news. Unfortunately, that is anything but what she received.

She had expected to be able to collect from her insurance policy which would enable her to retire. She had worked very hard as she performed the duties of a domestic, cleaning houses *all* of her life.

She always kept a watchful eye continually focused on her policy, feeling that some day it would be her passport to finally enjoying a well earned restful retirement.

She felt that the benefit she would receive, would give her the ability to afford to retire.

But, the policy that she had, was a paid up at 65 policy and was not to provide her with what she thought she had to retire on. Her policy would pay her beneficiary, in the event of her death. She did not have to make anymore payments on it, after the age of 65. However, she personally would receive absolutely nothing.

This devastated woman started to cry hysterically saying, "What am I going to do? I am all crippled up with arthritis and now I have to keep working until the day I die". She pointed her thin curvy arthritis ridden finger at Phil O'lies and said, "You know that you told me, if I took out this policy I would be able to retire. Admit it, come on admit it", she screamed as she shook her finger in his face. Her frail body shook uncontrollably. "What the hell am I to do now, huh"? ***"Oh, my heart**, I think I will end up having a heart attack"*!

Phil O'lies said "you need to calm down". He wrinkled his nose, looked over his half glasses and said, "I can't help it, if you just don't understand things".

It was a heart wrenching experience Adam thought, as he followed Phil out the door. Phil said, "Oh, screw her" as he slid his now shaking hand over his bald head and then proceeded into his luxury car. Adam wondered, is this the way **Mutual Of *Oh My Heart*** operates?

Adam wondered if Phil may have done exactly what he was just accused of, or if she really did misunderstand, at the time Phil originally sold it to her.

The testing for a State Insurance license is very intense. An Agent must have a State License. This should indicate that he supposedly understands and accepts the responsibility that is required. The object is to insure honesty and clarity of explanation. This is because Insurance can be very confusing to the novice.

Adam decided that he saw to many undesirable things from this particular agency that he felt was unacceptable, therefore he quit. He was then informed while giving his notice that he owed this Mutual Of Oh-My-Heart Insurance Company some money, because he was on a draw.

It took time to go through the classroom training, preparing for the State exam in order to get his State Insurance License. Then there was the timeframe that was required for the field training, during which time Adam wasn't making any sales at all. So, they claimed that he owed them quite a bit of money, because he was on a draw, all this time.

Adam could not get that lady that expected to retire, out of his mind. He was sure that she was correct in what she said about what Phil O'lies had told her at the time of contract.

Adam felt fairly sure of this because he too was sold a "bill of goods". He was told that he was getting a weekly salary and there was no mention of a draw, by Phil O'Lies at the time he was hired.

This should be a very honorable and respected occupation. The agency allowed someone like Phil O'Lies to continue to work as a manager for them, even though time after time these issues continued to come up.

[No you poor lady, you can't retire. You will have to work until you die]!

There was a class action suit brought against the Company by several Insurance Agents that were not told that they were on a draw. They all had been informed that they owed the Company money.

Adam was part of the class action law suit and found consolation in the fact that they won their case and ended up owing nothing.

Adam Fool felt that he was really was *a damn fool* for allowing Phil O'lies to sell him a bill of goods . . .

How ethical was this?

XIV. State Financial Insurance

We look in on this company that has set up a plan to "help" the new Sales Agents get up to speed. They would couple the new Agent with a seasoned successful Insurance Agent. The way it would work is as follows: the new Agent, who we will call Willy Makeit, was required to make most all phone calls for the seasoned Agent. Willy set all appointments for the seasoned agent who we will call Ceasar Agendas. Willy was expected to seize and set up Ceasar's daily agenda.

Willy had a very limited amount of time that he could use to set appointments for himself. He was given only a few hours per week to work on building his own client base. He was also expected to do all the filing and record keeping for Ceasar.

What did Willie get out of this? Ceasar was to guarantee the Agency that the monthly sales production attributed to Willy would be sufficient to support the salary for Willy.

This was to happen, even if Ceasar had to turn some of his newly acquired business over to Willy. Ceasar was to go on some of Willy's appointments with him as needed, and to be supportive. If Willy went on an appointment that turned out to be either too involved or in an area that Willy was not qualified for, than Ceasar would return to take it for himself. (Ex. Stocks)

In essence, Willy ended up performing almost as a personal secretary for Ceasar. He also changed hats to be Ceasar's telemarketer for the majority of the day.

This was set up by the Agency to allow the successful Ceassar more available time to close more clients; this was good for Ceassar and the Agency's ***bottom line***.

This however, was not such a good deal for Willy Makeit. He spent most of his time working for Little Ceassar and it did very little to build a client base for Willy. Willy really sold a bill of goods. Ceassar and the Company certainly enjoyed a good situation, but Willy had an undesirable situation and a disappointment in the possibility of a good future, that he had been told he could expect.

By now, you know, the drill, it is time to ask,

How ethical was that?

HOSPITALIZATION INSURANCE:

XV. Boot Cost Insurance Co.

This happened to a person we will call Seymore Bills. Seymore's wife unfortunately suffered many health conditions in her life.

In fact, she was in the hospital five times within the first six years that they were married. Unfortunately, Seymour Bills sure did see more bills that he had to pay, during his wife's lifetime.

It seemed that Insurance companies always found a way that conditions could be tied to some terminology, which would furnish them with the needed excuse to avoid paying benefits.

For one thing, it seemed that she was very prone to developing cancerous tumors in many areas throughout her body.

A perfect example of the "games people play" is when Seymour's wife had an ovarian malignant tumor. She was hospitalized and had the "diseased" ovary removed.

The following is a perfect example of the ridiculous excuse for Boot Cost Insurance Co. They actually used this excuse that would allow them to boot the cost to the insured.

They claimed that Seymour's group insurance did not cover maternity, even though he argued that this was not for maternity reasons. They said it was an organ that was part of the reproductive system. Therefore, Boot Cost once again was able to avoid paying and boot the cost over to Seymour.

Despite the fact that he continually paid the premiums, once again Seymour did see more cost obligation, booted to him.

Some insurance companies will do anything to avoid paying benefits and in essence boot the bill to you.

It may be that your policy doesn't cover that particular condition or you have and existing condition that will not be covered, or some other so called reason. We have come to refer to them as excuses.

This surely means, screw you today,
The chances are that you will find,
There is no way, the insurance will pay,
Just pay your premiums, on time!
How ethical is that?

DISTRIBUTING COMPANY:

XVI. Bogus Carton Company

We find a candidate who has sent in his resume to the Bogus Carton Company to which he received a response. They wanted to meet him at a local restaurant for a lunch interview. This type of interview is particularly uncomfortable because the one being interviewed usually ends up doing most of the talking. This will be done in response to the interviewer's questions. The outcome of this is that, the one who is interviewed can only watch his food sitting there. As soon as a bite is taken, you can bet that another question will be asked.

Well anyway, the Interview seemed to go very well for Woody Waite. Woody had extensive sales experience, but had never been in the Carton business before. [These Cartons are used for packaging with the each customer's company logo and name printed on them.)

The interview ended with Woody being told that Bogus wood definitely be in touch with him very soon. They said that they had some more interviews to conduct, but that they were very interested and that Woody should definitely hang in there. *[It sounds good so far.]*

Two weeks past by and Woody was about to climb the walls. He had sent a thank you letter for the interview, but heard nothing in response.

So, he called them and spoke with the District Manager that had interviewed him, weeks prior. Woody was told that he was in the running and (again) to hang in there.

It was took another two weeks before Woody heard from the Bogus Company and was then told that they had his references addresses but that they needed their telephone numbers right away. They needed to call the references as soon as possible, today! They were very emphatic. Woody called the secretary back within 15 minutes with all the telephone numbers.

She called back about an hour latter and said that they needed him to drive down from Virginia to North Carolina first thing tomorrow morning, to meet with the Management team.

Woody Waite headed to their location real early the next day, as he was sure that they had finally put this in high gear. He arrived one half hour early and enthusiastically walked in to the company office. He introduced himself and met with a surprising response. The secretary said, oh, did I neglect to tell you that they are at the local Holiday Inn.

After getting directions, Woody rushed to the hotel. He got there and quickly found out which room they were in. Upon calling the room, he was informed that they were in the middle of an interview and that it would be a while before they would be ready for him. He had already waited until the scheduled time, so as not to be too early before calling the room. He had to work hard in order to focus on remaining positive.

So, one and a half hours later, they called and had the desk send him up. Woody Waite went up to receive a very extensive interview. When it was about over, they told him that they would like to send him to their office in the Virginia area. They wanted him to meet the person who Managed that District office and shipping warehouse. This was very important as he would be working out of that particular facility.

Slightly disappointed, Woody headed home with hope, but he had nothing concrete as he had anticipated. He really had expected an offer. Oh well, at least they said that he would be hearing from them, regarding setting up the appointment for the visit at the company's Virginia facility.

Two more weeks passed with no call. So once again, Woody Waite called because, he was really getting tired of waiting. He had been told that they would be calling soon.

Now, it was over three months since the time of resume. It was about a month since the North Carolina trip. He had yet to have them make an arrangement to meet at the Virginia location.

Woody called again and said that it was now over two weeks since they last spoke and he told them that he now had another offer but would wait, if he was still in the running. He really wanted to work for this company. [He thought that he could make a success of it, if they would only get off the mark and make a move to hire him].

They told him, that they were not ready to make a move yet and couldn't give any advise as far as making the decision whether he should take the other job or not.

So Woody Waite just couldn't wait anymore. It was a couple of months since the rush, rush deal in North Carolina and the only contacts were the ones that he made. Woody moved on to another job.

About three years later, Woody ran into someone on the road at a restaurant. It was unbelievable that as they talked, Woody discovered that he had also applied to The Bogus Carton Company. He too, had driven to North Carolina. But, it was at a later date. He informed Woody that he hung in there for a while and that they had not hired anyone for at least two years that he was aware of. This gentleman was not hired either.

First of all, this was a very poor way to operate on behalf of The Bogus Carton Company. They should have put someone in that territory as soon as possible to maintain and possibly gain market share.

This was a good example where a company seems to lack the decision making ability, to settle on an important business decision in a timely fashion. One would wonder how many individuals did they string along, while they sat on making this decision.

Most importantly, if they felt it was not that important to expedite the replacement in that territory, then why advertise, interview and go through the motions.

They just jerked everyone around for no apparent reason. I do not really know what the hold up was all about or what went on behind the scenes. It was a shame that they didn't get their act together prior to pursuing a salesman.

So, it was ok to string these applicants along for as long a period of time as they chose to, and "piss on them, if they can't wait until Bogus was damn good and ready". Some applicants may have even given up another great opportunity from a real "legitimate" company.

How ethical was that?

MANUFACTURING COMPANY:

XVIII. Tighten DeValve Company

This is another interviewing experience with a company that sells large industrial valves throughout the United States. The Tighten DeValve Co. had called and made an appointment with Noah Trap, for the opening that they had for a National Sales Manager. The call was in response to the resume that Noah had recently sent to Tighten.

Noah was in the middle of the interview, when he was told that the owners and stock holders are very impatient. The business has not been good and they expect that, whoever is hired will be able to turn it around fast. Their salespeople are Manufacture Representatives and they may be pushing other lines more then the Tighten Valve Companies' line of valves. Of course, no other lines are allowed to include any competitor's valves.

Noah was told that he was expected to travel the United States and visit all Sales Reps. and then turn this sales situation around. Noah asked what time frame had the owners planned for this extensive turn-around.

He was told that they expected to see a marked improvement within two weeks.

Noah knew that he would not be able to have enough time to visit all Sales Representatives through out the USA, analyze which areas were in need of having his attention. He wouldn't have enough time to identify the areas of concern. Nor the time to be able to develop a plan, let alone implement the plan in time to turn this company around. Plus, at the same time, he would have to work on his own learning curve regarding product knowledge. Just allowing a two week turn around?

Noah informed him that he was withdrawing his name from consideration. He stated that their expectation with this short time frame, to accomplish this mission was unacceptable. It was certainly not in keeping with setting an achievable goal.

He knew that the Bogus Company would probably end up firing whoever they chose for National Sales Manager. No one could be able to accomplish this mission in such a short time frame to meet their expectations. For the Company to demand and expect success in accomplishing these energetic goals in such a short time frame, shows a definite lack off consideration, understanding, patience and most importantly, respect. This expectation is more like the impossible dream.

This business offer sure seems Bogus to me.

How ethical was that?

HVAC—HEATING VENTILATING & AIR CONDITIONING CO.

XIX. How's You're A/C Co.

The Sales Person is Garcia Opportunity. Garcia saw a lot of opportunity in selling maintenance service contracts to large chains.

He made phone contacts with many Corporate Headquarters. He then followed-up by the mailing of brochures and other info to the people that were in the procurement position. They were able to select the Companies that were to provide HVAC service contracts as well as many other services.

Most of the Headquarters were in other States. Garcia saw to it that they received an accompanying map that identified How's location. This was so they could see which of the stores, in their chain could take advantage of what the How's Company was able to provide to those stores.

Unfortunately, when working with Corporate Headquarters, you must accept the fact that it will take a while before a decision is made and the present contract ends with the present HVAC Company. The results could be a windfall for How's if they only wait.

However, once again this Company didn't have the foresight to be able to anticipate the huge increase in business, which would be the end results of adding these Companies to their customer list.

They sure didn't possess the patience to wait to reap the magnificent rewards.

Garcia had been able to build a great rapport with these people and would have been able to deliver, but How's couldn't wait. They laid Garcia off within a couple months of employment, so that if they were able to reap the harvest, they would be able to enjoy the whole enchilada. They would not have to pay Commission to Garcia for all his work.

This is literally out of the "book" of how to screw the salesperson.

Hear we go again.

How ethical was that?

A HAZMAT COMPANY:

XX. *HO-8-CHEM—Hazard Waste Removal*

The National Manager of this Company hired Pat Myback to locate the Super Fund Sites and coordinate the bidding effort for Ho-8-Chem for hazmat clean up. Pat was successful in locating these Sites as he used his personality for relationship building and organizational skills to discover additional prospects. But out of a clear sky, the Ho-8-Chem Co hired a man that was to replace the National Manager. The National Manager was sent packing and everyone that he hired also got the ax. This of course included our man Pat.

I don't know how much business the other salespeople had developed, but Pat figured that if the company played their cards right, they would have realized between eight and ten million dollars for his efforts. The new man was bringing his own people aboard.

Speaking of efforts, Pat received no commission on any of these which would have amounted to a huge amount at 10%.

Pat Myback didn't even get a proverbial pat on his back.

Pat was told by telephone that he was being laid off, as were all the other salespeople that had been hired by the previous manager.

How ethical was that?

THE FINANCIAL INDUSTRY:

XXI. Bank On The Shaft—Bank

In the last experience we saw where a new member of management was hired, which resulted in many layoffs, allowing him the ability to bring in his own people.

This is yet another example of the same type of situation.

We meet the **Bank Branch Manager** who has worked his way up in the company. We will call him Kent Survive. Kent was very much liked in the small city of only 25,000 people. Kent was a very low key type of a person with a good since of humor and an appearance like Abe Lincoln.

Kent belonged to many service organizations and clubs, where he was well known. This type of relationship building was certainly good for any business, and especially one in a small city.

Kent always made light of a life long challenge with his left leg. He had a limp due to a birth defect that affected that leg. You could always recognize Kent as he walked down the street, where everyone would call out to Kent, who they considered their "friend".

It seemed that he was always able to build business, due to the many people that did consider Kent a personal friend.

Then Kent received the bad news.

Kent's Regional Manager met with the chopping block. It wasn't long when his *new* Regional came in and said that he was removing Kent. He was bringing his own people because he was very comfortable working with them.

He wished Kent good luck, then turned around and just walked away as if Kent didn't even exist. Kent had no notice or any expectation of what just happened. He left with his head hanging, even though he had done nothing wrong.

Times became very difficult for Kent. He couldn't find a job because the only opening at that time was for a teller which couldn't produce enough income to cover Kent's bills. The other thing is that no one would hire Kent for a teller's position because he was over qualified.

Bank On The Shaft Co. had held the mortgage for Kent's home. Because it was also during a recession, Kent was unable to get another job in another industry. Now, the next step was that Bank On The Shaft Company wasted no time to send Kent a foreclosure letter.

The end result is that after the bank cut Kent's income, they then took his house. I wonder how they felt doing this to Kent, those damn heartless bastards. He had owned the house for ten years. That house held a tremendous amount of memories. The loss of not only the job but also the security of having a roof over his head had greatly affected Kent mentally. His teenage children grew up in that house.

Kent's wife wasn't very supportive. Despite the fact, that she knew it was not Kent's fault. She lost her house and couldn't live with that. There relationship was in great jeopardy, as was their marriage.

They moved to an apartment, but their lives and relationship were never the same. They eliminated his employment, took his home, took his sanctity, took his joy of life, and basically took his future.

How ethical was that?

By the way, why is it that if you have make a deposit at 9:00am on the 1st it will not be applied to your account until after 12:00am which will show up at 9:00am on the 2nd ? A deposit that you make after 2:00pm on the 1st.will not be applied to your account until after 12:00am the next day, and will not show up until the 9:00am on the 3rd. However, a check that you have written will be drawn out of your account just about immediately when it is received at the bank.

The money into your account will take up to 2 days while the money out of your account will be just about at once.

HOSPITAL CARE INDUSTRY:

XXII. Ain't A Merry Hospital

This is a true experience of a less than satisfactory Hospital stay. We all agree that most Hospitals leave a lot to be desired in regard to their attention to "customer service" and sometimes their attention to detail, as you will see in the following paragraphs.

The patient, Ima Patient was admitted in the hospital because of the failure of her recent double by-pass surgery. Her veins didn't hold up. This time she went into surgery where she was the recipient of a stent.

The next morning brought the welcomed sunlight. This allowed one to plainly view the extremely visible pollen, dust, and dirt clinging on the window. This was an older hospital and had a window that was capable of being opened. *[Note: A place may be old but it can be clean]*. Since, the window was open you could easily see the dirt and pollen also imbedded in the screen where it greatly restricted the fresh air flow that was trying to make passage into the room. I am sure that this has presented a major problem for those with an allergy or asthmatic conditions as with anyone in a weakened state.

One sitting in the room could plainly see the six blood soiled tissues that shared the floor with four straws and a lot of talcum powder. Ima had to lie flat because her groin area was weeping blood. This was due to the surgery and the amount of anticoagulants that her doctor had required she take on a regular basis in the years prior to the surgery.

The nurse finally got tired of waiting for housekeeping to come in and removed the debris, including some plastic tubing that had remained there overnight. She actively removed the items from the floor leaving the talcum powder conspicuously visible. The roommate had used an over abundant amount of powder, while in the bathroom of this semi private room. This resulted in footprints of powder being tracked from the bathroom, through the room and out the door of the room.

There was also the frightening danger of a needle and syringe sitting on the window sill, instead of in the infectious waste container that was conspicuously mounted on the wall.

The Nurse placed a cup of medications on the over-the-bed tray for Ima Patient to take. Since, some were of a generic nature, they were not readily recognizable. Ima Patient asked what the medications were, as she had already taken some of them the night before. She was only allowed to take certain pills, once in a 24 hour period. She didn't want to overdose.

The Nurse wasn't able to identify the medications and refused to take them to the pharmacy for identification, stating that they were too busy in the pharmacy to do that.

She barked sternly at the Ima that she could "take them or don't take them, that's up to you". Not only did she say this in a very sharp tone of voice, but she then stormed out of the room.

The Nurse had placed a sandbag on the patient's groin to control the bleeding, where they had entered to insert the stent. The patient's husband noticed that her groin was bleeding to the extent that her gown was covered with blood from the waist down.

He went out to the Nursing station and proceeded to request help for his wife. The one he was talking to told him, "you have to go to the other side of this station and tell them as I'm not a nurse". They were all standing within arms length from each other. The first one he told could, have turned around and clued the nurses in. Well anyway, after walking around the Nurses station the husband had to wait for the right nurse to come in and handle what could be a serious situation. You see the nurse had to be the one that was assigned to that room.

The Ima Patient's major concern wasn't the fact that they were not prepared to bring her first meal after surgery. It wasn't because they couldn't find an over the bed tray for her to eat her first meal from after the surgery. It wasn't that they didn't seem to care that they had left the previous patient's infomation on a board that was visible for all too plainly see. *[This was obviously, against the HIPPA regulations of confidentiality]*. Her concern was the fear of *infection*. No wonder there are so many cases of staff infection in hospitals today.

What kind of "Patient" care is this? What kind of a way is this to run a "battleship"? What a way to show good moral judgment.

How ethical was this?

XXIII. Primary Doctors

We will call him, Doctor Will Dolittle

[Working as a Doc in a Box]

This isn't about any one Doctor in particular. It is to draw attention to the way that most areas of our medical care have changed.

We are lucky when a Doctor will be able to see us sometime within this *century*. You must make sure you make an appointment at least a week before you get sick. *[Huh]!* When we finally get an appointment, we must remember that we dare not be late.

We will receive a fine if an emergency comes up, and we have to cancel so, make sure you call in advance. Yes, that's right, before you are aware that the emergency will happen, or you will be fined again.

> *[I don't know when I will be sick or have an emergency, because they keep back ordering my crystal ball, what's a patient to do]?*

> What if Doctor Dolittle changes your appointment? So what?
> What if the Doctor is late because of a golf game? So what?

Then you go to the office and have to sit in a waiting room, while other sick people continue to cough, sneeze and fart, filling that waiting room with enough germs to contaminate a small city. You can plan on extended exposure to these germs as you will be there for quite a while, trying to take shallow breaths and hold your nose. But then So what?

After you have waited long enough to read all the outdated magazines and the yellowed newspaper that probably has headlines reporting the end of World War II, You finally may then be called into the examining room. *[Wow! At least you're getting somewhere]*.

Now, that you have a change of scenery, you can expect to spend an amount of time up to an hour waiting without anything to read, but Dr. Dolittle's predominately displayed sheep skins on the wall. *[I wonder where he graduated in his class, probably rock bottom]!*

While you are waiting, the Doctor is running from room to room taking care of an assembly line of those that are sick, or hurt, and those that think that they are sick or hurt. *[Bring me that old yellowed news paper, I'll read it for the fifth time]*.

It makes you wonder how he is able to keep each one straight and not confuse the maternity case with the prostate patient. *[Oh boy]!*

But he is the Doctor.
You see, we now have managed patient care in effect.

Doctors have given up the so called private practice as we have known it. They have a collective practice where several Doctors share Receptionist, Secretaries and Nurses. Most blood work is farmed out as are the MRI, and X-rays. Patient management care associations only allow fifteen minutes per patient. *[This is hardly enough time to perform the work of a diagnostician, let alone be able to provide any necessary treatment. But this is the way to operate for the Bottom Line]*.

The following is a perfect example of cause and effect of managed patient care.

There was a patient that was experiencing a very trying situation, when her doctors found controlling her blood pressure a real challenge.

We will refer to her as Lucy Asicky. Lucy was going to Doctors at a place I will call, A Patient Hurts Medical Practice. They had her coming in weekly to have her blood pressure taken. This was followed by a review of her prescribed medication's performance. Although she religiously kept all her required appointments, she very seldom saw the same Doctor twice in a row. This frequency continued for at least two months, but proved of very little advantage. *[I think this was arranged by Dr. Bill Depatient]*.

One of the Doctors finally decided to send her to an endocrinologist to have her thyroid checked out, since there appeared to be some irregularity in a previous blood test.

Lucy was told by the Doctor of endocrinology that she was to have a mammogram, bone density and other tests. The real bomb shell was when she informed Lucy that she had developed emphysema. Lucy's husband said the doctor must be either a quack or she is sending business to other colleagues. Despite the fact that it seemed that she was probably getting a "kick back", it turned out, that was a wrong assumption.

This Doctor actually was the only one to realize that there was more wrong with Lucy than what she had been treated for. Lucy's husband had a difficult time trying to figure out how a "team" of Doctors were unable to realize that there was more to Lucy's physical health condition. They hadn't reached the conclusion either independently or collectively that there was a definite need to be more thorough.

Well, it turned out that Lucy only had one major problem, but that would prove to be fatal. She finally had decided to stop smoking after a life time of putting fire to anywhere from two to three packs of cigarettes per day, which she felt was something she couldn't do without. She had now made up her mind that it was about time to quit and actually stopped "cold turkey". Good for Lucy but, not good enough. She did stop smoking, however not in time. She stopped just two weeks before she was diagnosed as having emphysema by the endocrinologist.

Please note that she wasn't told by a lifetime of the Doctor's that she should stop smoking at anytime over the years. More importantly, she had no idea that she had emphysema and it certainly seems that her many Doctors didn't possess the aptitude to provide a proper diagnosis.

After a time of diminishing health, she reached the point where she needed to have oxygen piped into her bedroom. During her last visit to the endocrinologist her husband witnessed her saying, "Doctor, it must be difficult when you lose a patient". She then asked, after a slight pause, "Doctor, are you losing me"?

The Doctor stated, "Lucy I don't know, but whatever we are trying, just isn't working". Lucy was taken right to the hospital where she spent her final days.

We must remember that this whole bank of Doctors didn't have a clue. They gave Lucy the required fifteen minutes, which only allowed for the taking of her blood pressure. However, not scheduling enough time for a proper diagnoses for Lucy, allowed them to see more patients and add to the all important **Bottom Line**.

Congratulations Doctors, you were able to *take in more money*, while Lucy was only able to *take in* her *last breath*.

The decision to smoke was surely Lucy's fault, but not diagnosing and treating her condition, can only be blamed on a group of what we call Doctors.

How ethical was this?

Another Primary Doctor event

We now meet the patient, Mrs. Wanda Live.

This experience begins when Wanda was talking on the phone with her son. You see, Wanda's son, Will would call every day to check on his mother ever since his father died five years prior.

During the discussion Wanda mentioned that she was going to the local pharmacy, in this small suburb of a city in New York State. Will asked her why she was going to the pharmacy, to which she then replied to get her prescription filled for her bladder infection.

Will was very shocked in her answer, so he responded with, "do you mean that you have that again"?

He was aware that it wasn't unusual for someone to get a bladder infection every so often, but her answer further troubled him. She stated that, "no, I do not have it again, I have it yet". Her son quickly responded, "You mean that you have constantly had that problem for over a year"? Wanda said that was the case, and she has been taking the medication for the same period of time.

Will than asked when she was last to the Doctor. She indicated that she hadn't been back to the Doctor for over a year. She usually calls his office and the nurse informs the Doctor that she called. He has the pharmacy called to renew the prescription without ever examining her.

Will shows his disbelief and utter disgust in a Doctor ordering a prescription and not monitoring the results. He tells his mother that he will be right over and take her to the Doctor's office.

Wanda gets noticeably upset as she states that she doesn't have an appointment, so she can't go. Will than informs her that an appointment will not be necessary, since any Nurse can let her pee in a bottle and make sure that after a period of more than a year, this is the right course of treatment.

Much to the son's surprise, the result is that the Doctor still claims that she does continue to have a bladder infection. Finding this so hard to believe, Wanda's son made arrangements to take his mother to an Urologist to verify that this is, in fact a bladder infection. If it is, then it is the most stubborn case that most people have ever heard of.

The appointment was set and Wanda and Will were punctual in keeping the appointment. The Urologist examined her and took several samples consisting of blood and a urine specimen.

A few days later the Doctor called and requested that Wanda go to the hospital emergency room as an out patient. He wanted her to take some x-rays.

That evening when Wanda and her son returned to her house, they were greeted by a message on the telephone answering machine.

It was from the Urologist's office, requesting that Wanda return to the Hospital as soon as she could, to have a lung x-ray.

The next day Wanda returned to the x-ray dept. of the Hospital. When she was taken in for the x-ray, her son over heard a Nurse state "she is the one with the kidney problem". The Nurse left the area before there was any clarification on the meaning of her comment.

The next day Wanda and Will went to the Urologist for consultation. As they sat there, the Doctor hit them with the terrible results. Wanda did in fact have a problem with her kidney. What she didn't have was a bladder infection that she had been falsely treated for, over the last year. What she did have was a kidney that was plagued with Cancer. The Doctor explained that the Cancer had migrated to her lungs. This was not the news that they wanted to hear. Wanda didn't really understand the seriousness of her condition, as she half listened in shock to the Doctor's diagnosis. It seemed that either Wanda didn't comprehend or refused to comprehend what she really wasn't prepared to hear.

Will made contact with an Oncologist to see if there was anything at all that could be done with her Cancer. I will call him Doctor Ceasar Money. He brought him the x-rays and left very emphatic orders with the Doctor's Nurse. Tell Dr. Ceasar that if he can provide her with a quality extended life, let's go for it. But if he can only extend Wanda's life on this earth for a short time and in pain, then forget it. Will said that it must be a quality life or nothing. He told the Nurse that this is the way it has to be.

After going to Dr. Ceasar Money, Wanda went into the Hospital to have them see what they could do. Will waited for Dr. Ceasar to give him the information of his mother's prognosis.

The head Nurse told Will that he was to call Dr. Ceasar. When Will placed the call to the Doctor he said that he needed Will to sign a release so that he could start Chemotherapy. Will said that he would not sign until the Doctor gave him her prognosis. The Doctor said, "If you do not sign it, you will never know if **you** could have saved your own mother's life. When we start this, you will need a Nurse in your home to help her when she goes home". He sure put Will on a real guilt trip.

Later, Will went to the head Nurse and told her that he was very confused. He told her that every time he looks at his mother she looks terrible and he can't imagine that she will be able to go home. She has been continually going down hill. The Nurse told him that he was right, and although she didn't want him to let anyone know what she said, she doubted that his mother would make it past a few days.

Will asked, "Why would the Doctor say what he said, about going home and needing a Nurse"? The Head Nurse stated that she got in trouble once before when she advised a couple not to put an addition on their house for their sick mother. She knew that she, too, wasn't going to make it. They got very upset with her and wanted to believe Dr. Ceasar Money. "The Doctor told them the same thing that he told you". Their Mother died and didn't make it out of the Hospital alive.

Will said that he could see his mother going down like a ton of bricks, why would the Doctor say these things.

The Nurse said, I can only give you one answer, and as she spoke she brought her hand up between Will and herself and rubbed her thumb across her fingers. Will recognized that action as a sign that indicated money.

Yes, Dr. Ceasar Money was out to seize all the money he could get his hands on, even if it meant keeping a patient alive as long as he could so he could continually collect for Hospital visits. He did this, while giving the family false hope, just to continue to fill his pockets as much as he could for as long as he could.

How ethical was that?

XXIV. Production Print Distributorship

This company is run by a rare bird. I will call him Ed D. Debtpayer. Ed started his company and much to the surprise of many, he had an unbelievably successful initial year. Because of the success that started as early as his very first year, he quickly reached a point where it was time to bring on other salespeople. Unfortunately, as an honest and trusting soul, he did not require that they sign a non-compete contract. Instead he turned over his list of satisfied customers to them, so they could continue to take care of the customers while having some customer base to start with. I bet you can anticipate the outcome. **[If you thought that they would end up stealing his accounts for their own selfish good, then all I can say to you is, "damn you're sharp, You are absolutely right"]**. After they took off with a lot of his customers, the result was that Ed had to try to perform a fast step in order to save his business. Despite the loss of so many customers, he tried to still keep up with his bills. Unfortunately, he kept falling further behind.

There was a much easier alternative, if he would just declare bankruptcy and regroup. But you see, that was not Ed's way of doing things. He felt that this may help him, but it wasn't ethical to stick all his suppliers with his unpaid bills. So he took on the long journey of paying all his suppliers whatever he owed them. It was tough and it took years of sacrifice. Finally he had paid them everything he owed them. He was ecstatic. He could now smile and face the world, knowing that he had done the right thing. He did not "stick" anyone.

Now, he would call all those suppliers, and place some orders because he was in a solvent condition. He was feeling good about not sticking them with unpaid bills. However, his excitement was short lived. He was greeted with, "Big deal, you held us up all this time until you paid the bill. What do you want a pat on the damn back for finally paying up"?

He could have declared Bankruptcy and walked away. Since he had very little money, they would have received absolutely nothing. He had always remained in contact with them as he whittled his indebtedness down. You have to give him some credit! Just about every dollar he earned for years went to paying off his bills.

He *suffered,* by being too trusting of mankind when he hired salespeople without protecting himself. He *suffered,* because he wanted to give them a good start by turning over most of his business contacts to them. He *suffered,* because he chose to pay off his obligations to his suppliers rather then declare bankruptcy and walk away "Scott free". Then finally he *suffered*, when he was belittled by these same suppliers for taking so long to pay them. Ed was ***ETHICAL*** in what sure seems to be an unethical world. He tried to do the right thing. Ed D. Debtpayer was a debt payer, but received **no respect** for it.

So, for the last time in this writing, I will once again ask,

How ethical was that?

Chapter III

ETHICS:

(Ethics-*relating to morals, as per Webster*)

We have heard it referred to as the vanishing code of ethics. Is the code of ethics really vanishing?

There is awareness and a real concern as we can plainly view most corporations that are displaying so very little regard to ethical conduct. This serves as some evidence that maybe this is in fact a vanishing code. There use to be a very strong code of ethics, without saying.

So, this leads us to ask the following question;

Does the implementation of ethical values have a place in today's very competitive business climate, when it is combined with the serious concerns that exist in regard to today's economy?

It seems apparent that ethical placement is positioned last on the long list of business priorities, and that is only if it is taken under consideration at all.

In today's competitive market, every company must be compelled to evaluate their selling price and make adjustments accordingly. This we know is needed in order to provide the marketability of their services or products.

We realize that companies are very limited in the number of ways that are available for them to be competitive, while still being able to realize a justifiable profit. As a business, they sure cannot cut off the heat, air conditioning, and certainly not the lights. *[You know people are just so fussy, fussy about these things].*

There is a severe limitation to cutting supplies, as these items are, of course needed as a means for them to be able to do business.

[Sometimes they consider cutting down on the quality].

Example: In the production of refrigerators, when they come off the assembly line, most are produced with ripples on their sides. This condition could be virtually eliminated, however to accomplish this would require that they slow down the manufacturing line.

This would result in a boost in their cost and hence, that would be transferred to a relative boost in the selling price.

Since, the competition uses this same *express* method of manufacturing, then the company in this example would not be able to provide a cost effective way of competing, provided that they were in fact the only company that slowed their production line down.

Hopefully, the end user will be able to place their new refrigerator between their kitchen cabinets and maybe the ripples will not show.

[If they do not have the cabinet layout, with a design allowing for placement that hides the sides, I guess it's just tough nuggies].

So, Corporate America says, "let us forget concerning ourselves with this quality issue. As long as we just state that we have *high quality*, we can then hope that the statement in itself will suffice in allowing us to close the sale".

Hopefully, this will prevent further discussion regarding the ripples. The "buzz word", *quality* sure aids in the ability of closing the sale. Company representatives will tell you exactly, what you want and expect to hear, because it sells.

[We will discuss buzz words, in a later chapter].

How about the most flexible of all overhead cost? *Payroll*, oh yes, the company can either reduce the quantity of their employees or cut loose those *dedicated employees that have "over stayed" their* welcome for *too many years to be replaced with some that will work for less income..*

Most companies will think along these lines because, they consider that these long term employees are being paid *too* much money.

[Have you ever noticed any need for a Brinks' truck on payday for these long term employees? I don't think so].

Unless there are some CEO'S of major companies that are hardly making ends meet, how could they possibly harbor any feelings in regard to their foot soldiers? How could they relate to these people or care about their situation.

It makes you wonder what corporations are saying and thinking during meetings and while they are behind their closed doors. Let's identify some of the possibilities of their thought process or even statements they may make.

"Yes, let's get out the *chopping block!*"
"Do we really need this extra layer of management?"
"What do you think about these long term worker bees?
"Let's make some real cuts and realize some real savings".
"Big deal, maybe they have helped to make the company what it is. They did a great job in the past, but hell, that was then, we have already squeezed them like lemons, so now is the time to cast them aside. We need to have them, just go away. This will certainly provide a **positive** impact on the **bottom line,** if we can hire someone for less money".

[In other words, companies do not feel that they should save the last dance for the one that brought them there].

Companies may give the appearance that they're actually operating in an ethical manner. [Aren't they? Watch ya think]?

Some companies seem to constantly throw some *"crap"* against the wall just to see what sticks, even if only for a short while.

Less experienced candidates will undoubtedly work for a lot *less.*

Wow! What a savings! *Or is it?* Did they consider that those with less experience *usually* produce results that could mean a lot less of many things? **Less results** in workmanship, sales, service and maybe even dependability?

A Perfect example:

A well known Computer Company, let's call it Hybe-am Corp. was having a difficult time extricating their craniums from their anal orifice. Then finally seeing the light, they realized that they needed to make the necessary changes from the Mainframe to the Personal Computer.

Before the competition from minicomputers and then pc's, the Company was expanding beyond belief. Typically, an empty grocery store or other retail space would soon be converted to accommodate the overflow expansion of this computer giant.

This was accomplished by the removal of the shelves and gondolas and replacing them with the good ole' "cubicles" that we *love so dearly* and have become such a mainstay in the office setting.

[Yea, they make you feel just like you're at home, right]?

Well, in no time the space had lost its identity as a retail grocery store. The magic is done, and presto, we now have developed an extension of this computer co.

They even leased new buildings that had been constructed just for this computer company's use. It seemed that it would never end.

Now, there comes the unbelievable demand for the Personal Computer, which was a direct result of its more than expected, explosive popularity. Actually, the true extent of the demand was yet to be realized.

The well known giant had to make major changes or risk the loss of market share. This required a major change in mindset for the powers that be. It necessitated a change from the old Mainframe Technology of the past, to the cutting edge P.C. technology that was a design of the present, while setting the stage for great leaps to the future.

They had been losing market share in the Personal Computer business, which was like a fast moving train. They definitely realized that they were going to find themselves left stranded at the station.

During this time, they had an employee on loan to The United Way. We will refer to him as Hon Loane. Hon was working in a managerial capacity for a period of one year, during which time the Hybe-Em Computer Co. continued to pay his salary.

This was for, all intents and purposes, a donation to this great cause. When he returned after the year of assignment, he quickly learned that his previous position was eliminated.

[There is No surprise here, as we sure knew that this was coming].

The Computer Giant was after all, going through a metamorphosis from a Main Frame caterpillar to a Personal Computer butterfly.

Now, they had to look at the business of saving dollar$. How about getting out that *chopping block* and blowing off the dust. You see, they had *not* been in the habit of making personnel cuts.

In the past, if an employee showed up for work, he almost always was guaranteed a job, regardless of his production history. I honestly think that sometimes, it really didn't matter how willing to work or how capable they were, as long as they did in fact, show up.

The pendulum has swung in this regard, when compared to the way it was. Presently, everyone's productivity is where it is all that really counts.

So, Hybe-Em told Hon Loane, upon his return, that his new position at this time was to muster out these long term employees.

[At least, these employees were offered a buyout. Not all employees are fortunate enough to receive this kind of deal].

Hon was to provide them with their *"last supper,"* so to speak. Providing a meal and a quick thank you for their many years of dedicated service was the theme of the times. Then it was adios amigos, sayonara, arrivederci and don't let the door hit you in the ass on the way out. These employees must have suffered indigestion on this meal knowing that they were no longer considered needed, and that they were being cast away much like a pair of dirty old socks. They sure had been very useful and fulfilled the needs of the past.

Hon had to learn fast how to make these types of arrangements, as there were literally thousands of those dedicated employees who now had been selected to bite the dust. The company could use associates that would work for less remuneration.

Wow! What a savings! [Or was it]?

Let's fast forward a year. Oh, Oh. There seems to be trouble in Computer City. The *replacements* for these employees were *not* the *same* as the experienced tried and true dedicated employees of the past. *[Surprise, surprise. Who would have thunk]?*

They found that they can't just change one person for another. All workers really are not the same. How about that? Quick, get them back. At least they will not have to pay benefits, although they will be forced to pay them a lot more on a consultative basis, than when they were there as employees". That scenario is exactly what took place at Hybe-am Corp.

Note: My personal feeling is when we had used the terminology **"employees"** of a company; everyone felt that they were a part of that company. Goodbye to the term, **employee.** Now, we are just associates. We "associate" with a company until we move on or, most likely, they choose to send us packing.

> *[Where is that chopping block? It is not too far away and this you can bet on. It is used extensively in today's society. Chop, chop]!*

> *[Don't get too used to any place, wherever you work. Even the reference to full time, permanent, doesn't carry with it much permanency].*

If the choice to make a change is on the associate's part, it is usually because of anemic pay, inadequate benefits, or a less than tolerable work condition. Hopefully, moving on will be an improvement of one or more of these situations.

[Is the grass really greener on the other side]?

When people are cut loose, they usually do not get the buyouts, as the previous example company provided. A lot of these associates suffer from a loss of pay, loss of medical insurance and are left with mental stress and other health issues. Families are devastated, Marriage ties are unraveled and futures are destroyed. So what? Who cares? Certainly not Corporate America.

[Isn't there something morally and ethically wrong here?]

Let's look at another practice. Companies got in the habit of "writing up associates". I feel that writing an individual up multiple times has the same effect as spanking a child multiple times. After a while, it looses any impact and accomplishing nothing. It should only be used as an action of absolute last resort, if at all. We should write-up an associate only when there is a resistance to adhering to the company policies or the continued demonstration of a poor work ethic.

Writing someone up is usually done to provide the documentation needed to provide a company with protection from litigation. This is done in case the company decides to discharge them. The company would focus on obtaining three write-ups on the associate in the hopes of justifying their reason for cutting the associate loose. *[The three strikes you're out rule].* This takes place even though there may be very little rhyme or reason for writing them up, let alone a reason for discharge.

A company which I will refer to as, Hys' Building Supplies, was trying to prevent any loss of business. They instructed their department associates to help out at the registers when there were more than three customers in line. Hy's devised a system where they would announce something like a code 600 which would indicate that there was a need for associate from the departments to help out. In one instance, Kent Duboth, an associate from one of the departments did just that. Unfortunately, at the same time as he was helping at the register, a shipment was delivered to his department for Kent to put away. When he returned to his department it had been sitting there waiting for him. Kent was than written up, for not putting the shipment away in a timely fashion.

On another occasion he had to take a detour, while on his way to work. A hurricane had hit the area which provoked a neighbor into experiencing a health problem. This required the presences of many rescue vehicles causing Kent to take the detour. This gave Hy's another excuse for writing up Kent once again. *[You see, Kent was two minutes late. Wow that sure was unacceptable.]*

Kent was written up 26 times for similar BS. They haven't cut him loose as of yet, because he is a very good employee. You figure it out!

Usually, just a counseling or training session is all that is ever needed, unless a company is laying the groundwork for an eventual discharge. However, now it has become more prevalent to see companies lay off associates and actually tell them right out, that it is in fact, a cost cutting measure. They don't provide any other excuse for the layoff, as they did in the not to distant past.

They may be excellent associates, but they have just been around too long. They are paying them too much money as far as the company is concerned. Cost saving cuts must be made and these associates have become just the spoils in the competition war.

As long as the company can try to fix their ills on the expendable worker's back, why should the company care? Such *ethics!*

Maybe, they can make Wall Street happy. Who cares about these workers? They are insignificant in the broad scope of things.

This may be thinking out of the box, but I can't help but include the likening in complexity to what I proceed to state next.

Could we make a comparison between the magnitudes of the disintegrating good ethical behavior and this Country's deteriorating infra-structure? [*This is a little different comparison, I know.*] Both seemed to have been ignored for so long, resulting in an almost insurmountable task of repair.

Can we put "Humpty Dumpty," back together again?

This writer feels that we can close our eyes to either of these serious conditions, for just so long. The result of continuing to ignore either of these conditions can have, as a result, an equally harmful effect. The seriousness of either one, or the combination, could bring this great United States of America to its knees. We all realize that health care, cost of energy etc. could also accomplish this downfall and by no means is it my intent to minimize the possible catastrophic outcome of those conditions. The cost of infra-structure repair and the result of continued deterioration of ethical behavior by Corporations and Individuals alike could present a devastating cause and effect, beyond belief.

The continuation of used and abused associates will also take its toll. This will result in a monumental drain on the economy, because disgruntled associates produce less, and the quality may suffer. Remember, *action begets reaction.*

Watch for the resulting increase in product and service cost due to the possibility of lower production standards and reduced output. The cost will surely be passed on. I feel that this is slowly starting to happen.

Do you remember when we referred to Human Resources as the Personnel Department? This too had seemed to possess a personal connotation to it. Personnel Departments are now called Human Resources. The term Human Resources seems to lend itself to putting all kinds of resources in a similar category, whether there is a need for office supplies, a mop or even an additional associate.

[Should *associates be considered just like any other commodity*]?

The difference lies in which resource person will have the responsibility in the procurement of which commodity. The fact that the commodity to be acquired is a human does not seem to alter the fact that he or she is considered the same as any other item to be supplied.

Has the majority of Corporate America ever studied the effect personnel turnover has on a company? When you add the cost of training, to the loss of production, the costs add up to staggering numbers.

This is because "new" hires are usually either the *unconscious* **incompetent** or the *conscience* **incompetent**, in their ability to perform.

> *The Unconscious incompetent* doesn't know, but doesn't know that he or she doesn't know. *[Huh?]*

> *The Conscious incompetent* realizes that he or she doesn't know, but still must work through their individual learning curve.

In either case, they display a level of incompetence.

The result of turnover usually equals missed sales, poor customer service and diminished production. The associates past experience and the company's extent and quality of training, [or lack thereof] will obviously have a great bearing on the time frame required to get the new associate up to speed and capable of acceptable production.

Sometimes, it is better for the company when managers deal with an associate whose faults they are aware of, rather than going with a roll of the dice and taking a chance on someone new. They never know what kind of faults that the unknown might bring with them. They are disappointed quite often when gambling on new associates.

The success of a new associate actually starts at the interview. A quality interview can distinguish a good candidate that will give the company someone that they can mold into a good associate. Making the promising candidate become a productive associate requires the proper training and coaching.

It is a company's duty to give extensive training and this should be accomplished without prejudging that they may only be a short term associate. This way of thinking actually has a detrimental effect on the quality of training and will probably start the new associate off on the wrong foot. Short changing the training can result in almost certain associate failure, but by providing the proper coaching and follow-up supervision, the company will have set the stage for both a valuable employee and hopefully one of a much longer duration of employment.

The training and follow-up supervision will develop both the "existing" and the "new" associates. This will result in a degree of success that will provide *real* financial benefits both for the company and the associates. [**A Mutual benefit wow, how about that**]?

Yet, Corporate America seems to look only at instant gratification of supplying their stockholders with a favorable ***bottom line now***, ~ and the hell with the future. *[Associate hires seem to be a day to day thing without any retention or development planning, for the future].*

Yes, Companies *are* in business to make money, I have no argument with a Company making a just and legitimate profit.

However, let's see Corporate America show some concern and class for the sake of *all* concerned. *[I guess I must be a dreamer].*

I would like to see them show us how they can be ethical and produce a legitimate profit without the destruction of the employee and good business ethic alike.

[It may not be an easy challenge, but it is certainly possible].

Chapter IV

Terminology:

Mission Statement and Customer Service:

I note that most companies have developed a *mission statement.*

> Why not include an accompanying *Code of Ethics?*
> What in fact does this Company really stand for?

This should provide more insight as to whom they are as a company. This might, in fact, lend more credence to the *mission statement* itself.

> What about the word *service,* as it usually appears in most *mission statements?*

Customer Service:

"We provide good *customer service.*" We hear these words so much that it is no surprise that they have become buzz words. Maybe we should ask, "Compared to whom?" or "Compared to what standard?"

The word *service,* in the context of an offering of value, is probably one of the most used and abused of all words that we find ourselves exposed to on a daily bases.

What about those words, good customer Service? You will find "customer service" referred to in most Mission Statements, although it may be in an abbreviated form and appear as just the word "service" only.

I strongly feel that companies give a lot of "lip service" to the words "Good customer service". This is done In lieu of actually giving excellent, good or even an acceptable form of customer service.

The only choice seems to be between companies that offer, basically the same diminished type of service. Therefore, they can honestly claim that their service really is second to none. Thus, we experience the same poor service in every place we deal with!

Sometimes, you feel that the word *service* should be followed by some qualifying statement. These qualifying statements would serve *honestly*, as an explanation of what conditions would be necessary for the company to be able to perform their stated quality service.

The following fictitious exercise will, at least, lend itself to providing you with the type of conditions that would have to exist for a company to be able to provide service that will be to the customers' satisfaction.

This is a spoof that spells out the justification for providing the service that the company proclaims it provides.

> *[The following spoof actually gives the real reasons you may never get to experience good service even though you will not be told this].*

The company's pledge: We will provide you with *good service, provided* one or more of the following exist:

A. If the *bottom line* has enough profit built into it that will permit good service.
B. If the *scheduling* of personnel is sufficient enough to provide the desired service to fit your needs.
C. If the *time* available is conducive to providing the good service that you expect.
D. If we possess the *organizational* skills necessary to be able to "fit" you into our schedule.

E. If we have provided associates with the necessary *training* needed to give them the knowledge and ability to provide the kind of service that you both expect and deserve.
F. If your idea and our idea of good service actually coincide.
G. Etc.

Although, these qualifying statements are never stated by the company, they are indicated here to illustrate possible reasons why we experience such a severe lack of good quality service at a lot of locations. This **lack** of quality service exists, not only within retail sector, but also within the so called service companies.

[It sure gives you that warm fuzzy feeling, doesn't it? Not!!!]

Why then, are these companies successful? Why hasn't each industry self-corrected its own *"soft"* service condition? The answer is very simple. We live in an age of MEDIOCRITY.

Mediocrity is apparently the average standard to be measured by. How low do we allow our expectations to go while considering it still acceptable? Where do we draw the line?

No one company has a lock on giving *lip service only*, to the *claim* that they are providing good service.

I perform various types of employee training. Frequently, I get the opportunity to provide training in the real meaning of **Customer Service Excellence.** *The employees learn to perform beyond the customers' expectations. This proves to provide a huge benefit to the Company with increased sales as a result.*

Even though I am a true believer in Customer Service Excellence, I'm sorry to say that I find it almost impossible to discover it actually being performed at most locations.

There is so little real choice between the many companies that offer relatively the same anemic kind of service. Therefore, they can truly state that their service really is second to none. They are correct in this statement since it is basically the same caliber of service. UNEXCEPTABLE in a most cases!

The Mission Statement and Consultants:

A large number of companies probably would not have a mission statement at all, if it wasn't for the existence of business consultants. Many business consultants have advocated a mission statement. The inclusion of a line about "service" will usually be part of it. They are telling the customers what they want to hear which may not necessarily be the way it really is or what they will actually receive.

> *[They say that the definition of the Business Consultant is: One who methodically borrows a watch from one of the Company's Managers. Because of a Consultant's expertise, they will be able to present the Company with the precise time, at that exact moment. Of course it will be easier for a Consultant to decipher the time if the watch is of the digital variety. Ok, shame on me, for that one].*

Note: I do not take issue with having a mission statement, but rather with the validity of its content as it relates to the performance of each individual business.

I wonder if some of the company's principals are able to recite their own Company's mission statement without reading it first. Some might even be mildly surprised to learn of its content. Enough said in regard to the word service. I will conclude by saying, "if you do **not** expect *customer service excellence*, you probably will neither be pleasantly surprised or sadly disappointed".

> *[The customer in a restaurant states, "I would like a little service here!" The waiter replies, "Sir, you are already getting a little service. In fact Sir, you are getting very little!"]*

Let us not forget that Customer Service Excellence is dependent on the Company having good customer service policies in place. This must be combined with properly trained personnel, to be able to successfully follow thru on those policies with all their customers and clients.

Remember, this only comes with the proper training and continued coaching by the management team. Customer Service Excellence on a broad scale is possible, if the company doesn't lose focus in the realization that there is a need of continued dedication to make it happen, and it is definitely in the best interests of the company.

I will discuss our dealings with whichever name the company decided that the individual is to be referred to as: associate, sales associate, salesperson, clerk, sales agent, sales consultant, sales representative, or sales engineer [whatever?] later on, in more detail.

Quality

Quality always had been a factor that differentiated companies from each other. You know, you get what you pay for. *In the past you wondered where the yellow went?* **[Do you remember the old Pepsodent Toothpaste commercial?]** *In the present we wonder where the quality went.* It seems that the quality has been sacrificed to bolster the **bottom line.**

Quality control is presently more forgiving and seems to be nonexistent in too many cases. Have you noticed that when purchasing products from the same manufacturer multiple times, that the consistency, flavor, strength, color, or alignment is changeful?

[This is a mouthful, but the truth.]

Even your local newspaper appears to have dispensed with their proofreaders. Or maybe, they are just not as thorough as they seemed to be in the past.

I have been informed by a manufacturing company that "it is better to sacrifice some quality and get the business. Providing a better product or service might possibly mean sacrificing the chance of getting the business in lieu of maintaining the price competitiveness."

It is hard to believe that, despite the fact that quality can mean a degree of excellence, that there isn't a market for this higher standard.

To what degree has the consumer changed to accept a diminished quality or service in exchange for a reduced price?

Did you ever go to a party or any gathering where there was a group of people and hear anyone state that they made a purchase that was of the best quality? More likely, you would have heard them comment, "Boy, did I get a buy", "What a deal!", or "I practically stole that item."

Remember, when we were told when starting a new job that it was accuracy first, speed would then follow. Today, all we hear is

production, production and more production. There seems to be very little if any emphasis on accuracy.

Price:

Well certainly, if we have sacrificed service and / or quality, than we would expect the price to be much lower. Right? Contrary to most logical thinking, this is not necessarily true. A lower sell price will have a negative impact on that all important **bottom line.**

Even though there are lower dollar requirements in providing a lesser quality product and / or a mediocre service, the sell price has remained disproportionately high, in many cases.

Once again, since most competition basically read from the same book [so to speak], they can all truly state that they are "very competitive."

[A customer states "ABC Meat Market's price is $3.75lb for pork chops that you are getting $4.25lb for. The XYZ Company's representative asks, "Then, why didn't you buy it there?" The customer tells XYZ that the ABC store was out of that product at the time. To which the XYZ representative quickly interjects, "when we are out of pork chops, we only charge $2.50lb."]

Chapter V

Sales "Buzz" Words:

The term buzz word helps to differentiate between competitors.

We are different because ~~~~>

Most companies try to show why you should buy their product or service and it may even have to do with justifying the fact that their price is higher than that of the competition. A reason to do business with most companies must be devised to differentiate themselves from their competition.

Some of the buzz words have been used so much, that if they are not stated we may feel that something is missing, or we're being cheated.

1. Value Added Service:

This is another attempt to show that you are getting more value than you actually are paying for, hence the higher price.

> *[This is fantastic because you might even be offered the service you should have been getting right along].*

2. Quality:

This word has become a buzz word since it carries so much weight in helping a consumer decide on which item and where the item should be purchased. Because of the better quality it cost more. **[OK, you say so].**

3. Cost effectiveness:

These buzzwords are an attempt to make a comparison of apples to apples, so to speak. However, this will allow for price justification.

Example—"This item may cost a little more, but it will last longer, perform better, or will be easier to use, etc.

[Sometimes, you feel that you need a "Philadelphia lawyer" to evaluate a comparison of items, just to determine the best product for you, while taking everything into consideration.]

Today, it is a monumental task to select a provider of products or services, whether as an individual consumer or business entity.

We not only have an over abundant amount of competition, but an unbelievable variety of products to choose from. You can find this situation very confusing, requiring a great deal of consideration, in regard to product selection.

4. Sale:

When we see this in advertising or on a sign, we assume that it means that the item is at a lesser price. Actually, it really means that the Company has this particular item for sale. We have been condition to expect that the item will be at a greatly reduced price. This one word usually draws a lot of attention and hence ends up moving product.

5. Percentage Off:

This has the same effect as the sale sign, and provides the consumer with a savings off the original price whether it be suggested list or the Company's own regular retail price.

6. Bogo or Two For:

Either of these terms refers to the fact that if you buy one, than you will get and additional one free. The term "bogo", or buy one get one has been used in the retail industry for many years internally. This was used for identification purposes as to the type of sale. This is a term

that is now being used also to include buy one and get the other one at half the price.

7. Coupon:

This is a paper form that when submitted at the time of payment will allow the coupon holder to receive a reduction in the original selling price of the item or service.

8. Rebate:

This is similar to the coupon but usually requires the Consumer to mail this paper form in to the Company or the Manufacturer. There has been some very extensive studies that have shown that a large percentage of consumers do not mail the rebate forms in. Thus the company can appreciate a windfall by selling their product at the regular or list price. Most of the time there are strict rules that one must comply with, like sending in the original receipt that shows proof of purchase or by including the product bar code.

This is only a small example of some of the common buzzwords that we are familiar with and which we come in contact with, on a regular basis in retail etc. They have been included to give some what of an idea of what they are, how they are used and why they are included. Note that most of these have to do with the effect on the price.

Chapter VI

Competition:

Let's look at personal competition.

We live in an extremely competitive world. It starts in child day care and than carries through all of an individual's life: Day care, Grammar School, High School, College, Graduate School, Job Placement, employment position, and hopefully the competition for a possible promotion.

By the way, if you happen to be in need of an organ transplant, you guessed it, you are in competition again. Only in this case, it goes by the seriousness of your condition, at the time. If you show some improvement, than you drop down on the list. You still may be in need of a transplant, but you will just have to wait longer.

> *[Wow! There surely is a long intense competitive adventure to life, isn't there]!*

You must be in a competitive situation for personal production, sales production or the type of personal service you offer, just to remain employed.

You must be aware that there might be someone able and willing to perform the duties of your job, while working for less.

Associates willing to work for less probably will be much more palatable to your Company even though the results may not be as good as the results that you provide.

The Company may be tempted to make the change to save dollars. *They will basically tell you, "Goodbye, it has been nice knowing you".*

Now, we will discuss competition from a business standpoint. We all remember the old advice given to prospective entrepreneurs prior to opening a business entity.

They were told the three most important requirements needed for success: [it is not, money, money, money although very important.]

It is #1.Location, ~ #2.Location ~ and of course ~ #3.Location

This referred to the fact that you were bringing something new to a location thus fulfilling a need. In the days of old, this meant you had a real good chance of success.

Having something new that would fulfill a need, in itself, could *almost* assure success. This was provided that you possessed some entrepreneurial spirit, managerial savvy and a good supply of capital. [It is too big a gamble, if you are under capitalized.]

Location was so important, that it held the top three positions in importance.

Today, location—location—location seems to mean that if there isn't *already* a location—location—location of a comparable business, than you probably should not consider this particular type of business adventure or else, change locations.

They say [whoever *they* are] that competition is good. However, it seems we purposely continue to cut the proverbial business pie into smaller and smaller pieces.

I witnessed a perfect example in the fast food industry. I came across a stretch of highway were there are two fried chicken franchises separated by a hamburger establishment smack dab in the center. The property line of each one is common with the other, so that you are able to literally stand with the one foot in the parking lot of the hamburger place, and the other foot in the parking lot of either one of the franchised chicken operations.

Depending on which side of the hamburger's parking lot your one foot was placed, would than indicate which one of the chicken franchises the other foot would land in.

[This is what I call close competition.]

Okay, so what do you think that the hamburger operation decided they should add to its menu?

You guessed it, CHICKEN. Yes the same CHICKEN you could get on either the left or the right of this hamburger place. Now you are able to get fried chicken at all three establishments in a row.

[Why? I just don't get it! Does this make sense to everyone except me, or do you also question the reasoning behind this move]?

By the way, these were all national chains with names familiar to everyone, who eats at fast food establishments. *[That probably will include everyone except five people].* It is true, that as it turned out, they were not successful at all and after their trial run, the hamburger franchise ended up discontinuing the trial of selling chicken.

[Surprise, surprise, what were they thinking? Maybe, they just were not thinking.] I certainly can understand if you have a similar product that you hope to market. But, somehow, you have to find a way to differentiate yourself from all of your other competitors. Especially, if they are well established and only an arms length away.

On a larger scale, we see a similar competitive situation in all types of industries with little real difference between the players.

Take the ladies clothing industry, for example. You can find as many as six stores in the same mall that carry very similar or even the same exact items, with many produced by the same manufacturer.

The kicker is that most of these stores are probably under one big umbrella, sharing the same parent company.

Chapter VII

Sales People:

They may be referred to as Sales People, Sales Clerks, Sales Agents, Sales Associates, Sales Consultant, Sales Representative, Sales Engineers or just plain Associates. Let us realize that they are referred to by many titles. More important than the titles, is the distinction between someone who is a true Sales Professional and one who is an "order taker". A true Sales Pro sets the stage, creates (or establishes) the need and then follows through by closing the sale. While the order taker either writes down or rings up whatever the customer has already selected.

A great number of Sales People have had their credibility come under question, and rightly so.

Sales People have lost a lot of their credibility along with many other Professional people in regard to the way that they are viewed in America today. (Other examples are Doctors, Lawyers, Insurance Agents, and even Bankers.) They seem to be viewed in the same light as the proverbial "car salesman" was viewed a few years back.

[You know, would you buy a car from this person]?

In the past, sales people developed a lot of product knowledge. You might say that they knew their products inside and out. They also knew their competition inside and out as they also knew their competitor's products.

There have always been some sales people that earned an undesirable reputation, because of the objectionable individual's style or the approach that they had used, and the way that they made their presentation. We are cognizant that this has been true anytime throughout history.

We also realize that some companies actually promote the omission of information or the use of "selective terminology". This is done to allow the sales person to circumvent or avoid actually answering certain objections or questions that could produce a negative response. They fear that these negative answers could have the unwanted effect of "killing' the sale. Most of the time a tract *[or canned speech]* is used just for the previously described purpose. Tracts were developed mainly for the purpose of providing a vehicle to allow a good sentence and topic flow, but sometimes a tract is also used to cover up the lack of product knowledge on the part of the Sales Person. *[This is especially true when they're new salespeople].*

Some Salespeople will use terminology that is specific to the particular item that they are selling where they may not possess enough knowledge or understanding of the true meaning of that terminology.

As we look back in time, Sales People did most of the talking and the "prospect" did most of the listening. Today, we have the advent of "need selling". This is a good thing! The professional Salesperson questions, and then he *listens*. He is performing the fact finding phase, while the prospect answers questions and is doing most of the talking.

It has been stated that we were born with two ears and only one mouth, so maybe we should use them in the same proportion.

> *[Actually an 80/20 percentage ratio would prove most successful].*

The lack of listening intently by the salesperson will result with the salesperson being unable to provide the right answers and product selection that will satisfy the prospect wants and needs.

Addressing a need with a product or service is much better than walking into a prospect with a product or service to "push". This is without any regard to whether there is an actual need on the part of the buyer. Also, it is done without understanding the buyer's deciding factor, based on his need, as to which would be the proper choice for the salesperson to sell.

The problem is that many salespeople selling to the need have only surface knowledge of their product or service, that he or she is trying to present.

Salespeople need to address any objection immediately, and this can only be accomplished if they are listening.

Unfortunately, employers today do not want to appropriate the monetary investment needed to provide adequate training. This is because they feel that the employees will not stay with then very long.

You have often heard it said that, "knowledge is power".

The presumption that providing the necessary properly structured training will cost the company money is hurting our nation's ability to hone sales skills to a fine science.

This science of selling can reap rewards by producing additional sales and most likely will produce satisfied customers, thus promoting **repeat customers.** They feel that they were satisfied in the past, so that there should be no reason that they shouldn't enjoy the same good experience as they did then, when they require an additional item or service.

[This can also translate in less returned merchandise].

Just imagine the sales power that could be derived with the power from having the *knowledge* combined with the skillful use of *need selling* presented by a **well trained skillful salesperson.**

That would be powerful!

The Non-compete Contract:

The non-compete clause is very important protection for the company, in order to avoid the theft of their existing customer base.

The salesperson's point of view in regard to the Non-Compete Contract is that, this can complicate any Job change. If a Sales Person desires to leave his / her present employer, or he meets with the chopping block, he must make a decision on one of the following unacceptable alternatives:

#1. Wait out the period of time designated by the non-compete contract before re-entering the same industry.
#2. Move outside the territorial boundaries that are identified in the contract.
#3. Enter a completely new industry.

Most Sales People do not have enough saved up capital to be able to hold out for #1 and their family ties make #2 difficult. #3 is equally difficult as most companies require experience in the company's particular product line or service.

I witnessed a salesman that sold *caulking* material, who was going for an interview. He was told that he did not possess the experience in the particular *type* of caulking that the interviewing company sold, so the interview was cut short. You can bet that this was the end of the story on *that* job.

Chapter VIII

Business Development:

How did these corporations come about?

The overview of the usual *Steps of business development:*

1. **Idea stage—**
   The viability of the idea is investigated. Information is gathered on financial requirements, possible locations and the names of possible suppliers. Projections are made and a feasibility study is established.

   [Such a business, I should make a bundle. Hello Brinks truck].

2. **Established entity stage—**
   The business plan is discussed. Initial financing is arranged. Doors are finally open for business. You are lucky if you are able to pay your suppliers within 90 days.

   ["Was I crazy or what? I should have had my head examined"]!

3. **Survival / struggle stage—**
   Marketing and *long* hours are in high gear. You are still below the break even point.

   ["I am out of my mind, a real glutton for punishment"]

4. *Successful existence stage—*
Actually showing a profit and drawing a salary. Now, it is time to schedule an increase in marketing and / or to hire more sales people.

[I knew it would be a success all the time. Those fools that said I couldn't do it, they should see me now].

5. *Blast off stage—*
Owner's roll is more Presidential, and he has delegated managerial responsibilities. He hires a Sales Manager. Business appreciates excellent expansion. It may even be listed on stock exchange.

["What do all those nay Sayers have to say now?"]
["I sure showed them!"]

6. *Maturity—*
We now have a stable establishment. Acquisitions may be a consideration.

[Now may be the time to consider a business continuation plan, It is time to get out, kick back and enjoy the rest of my life).

The preceding overview was indicated here to illustrate the complexity of getting a business entity off the ground, even when it beats all odds and is actually successful.

So, has business forgotten what got them to this point? A better idea, better product, better selection, better service, or a better price, but let us not forget the conscientious, dedicated employees, that were there to help our businesses succeed.

Most likely, it took a combination of all of the above to play such an all important part in the success of the company.

It took perseverance, and tenacity to hang in there, and because you have paid your dues, you have earned the right to succeed.

It took a lot to get here and I don't think that our memories should be so short sighted, that we forget who helped it happen. How about those ethical considerations necessary and in place during the past, as the company was developing?

Despite the tough going to become successful, many companies seemed to developed amnesia, when it came to recognizing those dedicated individuals that helped to bring success to the company.

There are too many cases where the loss of employment seems to be the only reward that many employees received.

Chapter IX

Discrimination:

This chapter is included because discrimination is so prevalent, despite the fact that we are more knowledgeable today, and therefore should have more awareness and less tolerance of this deplorable practice.

We use to look at discrimination as just a crude unflattering recognition of racial difference. Actually, there are many differences that are subject to acts of discrimination.

The following will indicate some of the things that differentiate individuals from each other;

Our background, where we came from: people may be raised in the North, South, East, or West. How about those from other Countries all over the World?

The way we speak: We have different ways of talking: we speak with a drawl, use of slang, display an accent, have an inherent dialect, talk with a brogue and speak in many different languages.

Some people are *right handed*, some are *left handed*, some may have a handicap and some may have some other type of physical or mental challenge.

Our eyes are not the same: we may have brown eyes, or blue eyes, maybe even hazel colored eyes. Some may need corrective lenses, contacts, possess a glass eye or may not be able to see at all.

Some people have *hair* on their heads, sporting many different styles, or colors, facial hair, and hair on other parts of the body. Some may have no hair whatsoever.

Some have an extensive *education*, from any of a huge variety of schools, while others have little to no education. Some are self taught and some have gone to the school of hard knocks.

Some are *tall*, others may be *short*, or are thin while others may be heavier.

Some are *young* while others have been around for a *longer* period of time.

We are *men* and *women* with different *sexual preferences*.

As you can see, there are a lot of areas that prove that we are all truly **unique**, in the many ways that differentiates us from each other.

It is truly a shame, that **discrimination** in the **work place** is alive and well.

We can see it and feel it, in **other places** as well. Employers may advertise that they are an equal opportunity employer, but the problem can still lie with their managers or even the human resource department itself.

Classified ads will state that you must have a certain amount of experienced which narrows the search by cutting out the younger worker. Must be experienced, but no one is willing to give them the opportunity to gain that needed experience.

The same is true for the older worker. In their case, the classified ads will state that the applicant must be a recent graduate or have two or three year's experience, [*only*].

Rather than being open to all applicants, they know that they want to satisfy their bigoted way of thinking. They will advertise in a way which will allow their company to narrow the field down, to fulfill their prejudice. This can be accomplished without actually asking age or date of birth.

You may not be hired or even considered because you went to the "wrong college", [not theirs] or you may be too tall, too short or you do not comb your hair to their liking. We never know.

We may not get a promotion for exactly the same kind or ridiculous reasons.

BE PREPARED, BECAUSE DISCRIMINATION IS DEFINITELY ALIVE AND WELL. [No resuscitation needed for discrimination to live on]. We need to find a way to join together and bid a final good bye to any shape or form of discrimination. When a company has a suspicion that someone in your employ harbors some discriminating views, they must be dealt with quickly, directly and without toleration. Is a racial, religious, gender, etc. joke allowed to be told, at someone's expense? Enough is enough! ***Let us end it now!***

Chapter X

SUMMARY;

My message to our American Government:

You too need to take a good look in the mirror, Mr. President. You are duly elected to Protect, Honor and Defend the Constitution of the United States.

The *defense* [security] of our *great country* is your most important responsibility. Spend the time needed to accomplish that mission as opposed to wasting time focusing on the *defense* of the desires of *your* particular *party.*

Congress, together with the **President,** the two of you must **shuck** the whole **partisanship Bull Sh-t.**

Try **working together,** and do this while learning a lesson in the art of compromise. Accomplish what is *best* for our *beautiful country*, irrespective of party affiliation, personal agendas, and void of discriminatory considerations. Do this **without partiality** to any *single* Religion or belief.

We are the **United States of America** and United we will stand if you do your part to bring this glorious country **together.**

Listen and you will hear the concerned voices of the people that you are supposed to represent.

You are not there to preside as **dictators**, or in office just for your **place in history**. Remember, you too must follow the Constitution.

This may be a shock to you, but it really isn't about you.
The part *about you* **stopped,** at **your election.**

It is **about** the **American People** that you represent. Somehow, this fact seems to have always been forgotten.

Hopefully, you will learn how to **work together**, and although a decision may not be as pleasing to a faction of you own party, you must ask yourself if it is this best for the majority.

Remember that together we stand, and this means all of you.

If anyone of **you cannot** learn how to **work together** for the common cause, **[The American People]**, then maybe **you need to step aside** and let someone who understands this principle replace you!

How about trying ethical behavior in Government Too?

A Message for the Consumer:

Now there is a message to all of us, the consumer. We too must share in the blame as there is definitely enough blame to go around, unfortunately as far as the retail industry goes; they really have created a monster.

We, as consumers are not happy with a 20% savings. If we are not able to enjoy a 50-75% savings, we don't feel compelled to make a purchase.

So, what did we get?

We wanted **cheap** and we have succeeded by getting cheap. How many items have we purchased that were of **good quality? (Consider lead paint, products that poison children or don't last, defective products in many ways, etc.)**

It has taken many years to have diminished the manufacturing segment of this country to today's meager existence. We *helped* by the use of our purchasing power, to **send American jobs overseas.**

If we were not so focused on getting a "steal," than maybe, just maybe we would have been able to purchase better quality items that were actually made in the USA. How about the jobs we might have been able to save?

Maybe having a higher amount of domestic competition (before there was foreign competition) would have developed a just and more palatable price on these better quality items that were made right here.

We would love to welcome back the quality, **made in USA label! Who knows, with China experiencing their current difficulties, this actually could happen.**

Yes, Mr. and Mrs. Shopper, you are the catalyst that has *helped* Corporate America send jobs overseas. They could now be competitive, and be able to get market share, while saving you mucho dollars.

The ethical nature of Corporate America has been in decline. It may not be clearly defined as to where it all started, but we as consumers certainly have to share some of the responsibility for the part that we played in the diminishing, of CORPORATE AMERICA'S ETHICS.

As employees, we must protest the abuses that have been illustrated in Chapter II, but do it collectively. We know that there is safety in numbers. "Tell Corporate America that we have had enough"!
These abuses can only happen, if we allow them to happen.
Remember that, together we stand!

My message to Corporate America:

Well, since the premise of this book is about you, I certainly have a lot to address with you.

There are many Companies in Corporate America that do operate in a very Ethical manor. They provide excellent customer service and know the value of providing good associates with respect and a compelling place to work. This is evidenced by Fortune Magazine's 100 best places to work.

We see the correlation between how associates are treated and the quality of Customer Service rendered in a book titled, *"The SERVICE EDGE*, by Ron Zemke and co author Dick Shaaf. This book covers 101 Companies that profit from Customer Care.

The success of small companies found in the book *The Alpha Dogs* shows how these Companies have become the leaders of the pack by providing great Customer Service.

We recall the story of the owner of the manufacturing company in Massachusetts who addressed his employees after a devastating fire destroyed the building that housed their business and placed of employment. As he stood tall in a field of employees, he surprised everyone with his statements. Despite the fact that there was no way that the employees would be able to return to work anytime soon, he assured these dedicated employees that they would not suffer from the misfortune that destroyed their place of employment.

He stated that their income would continue for as long as it would take for their building to be reconstructed. The result was that when these workers finally returned to work they did so, even more dedicated while providing increased productivity and you can be assured that this would be void of any appreciable amount of turnover.

Whatever the future of this Company, its owner stood up for his dedicated employees in an unbelievable Ethical and caring manor. I can only hope that his generous act will be rewarded and may he always be blessed with all he endeavors.

Now, do any of the included case histories strike a familiar note with you? Do you feel honor or shame when you recognize that you may have been represented between this book's covers? In my estimation, shame and guilt should be written over your face, if you have not been supportive for your associates, providing good customers service and operating in an ethical manor?

Don't you know that operating a successful business while using good ethical conduct, shouldn't ever be considered an oxymoron? I can only say, shame on you, if you can't see the light.

Today, there are not as many people getting promoted, so upward mobility has all but disappeared. One of the reasons for this is that very few are around long enough. However, it seems that if you do receive a promotion to Corporate, you forget all the things you use to frequently complained were wrong with the way "Corporate" operated.

Now that you are there, you seemed plagued with instant "brain death". You not only read from the same book, or the same chapter, but the same page and paragraph. You are acting just like the Politicians that fall into the same rut. You complain that their needs to be change, but then what do we witness, only more of the same.

Wake up and *treat* and *train* your associates, and do it well.

This is the *true way* to have a positive impact on the bottom line.Evaluate what you are spending on turnover. Cut it out! There is a time when you need to weed and feed. Weed out the dead wood and feed with better quality associates.

Then have a good quality training program in place, and most importantly, *use* the damn thing.

You should **never, ever**, replace an associate for the **sole reason** to **cut expenses, while hiring one you can get for less!** Evaluate whether the Company really is better off because of that employee.

Let's **do away** with so many examples of the **"Peters' Principle"** by not promoting people to a point of their own incompetence. It's definitely your job to be responsible, so damn it **train them!**

> *[As a warning, remember that all those that are good Sales People may not necessarily make good Managers].*

Set the foundation for a great tomorrow, where associates are treated as valued employees again and watch the change.

THE SIMPLE FORMULA

Quality interviews will equal **quality hires** and with **quality training** of those hires you will then **produce quality employees.**

Then by taking **an interest in them, t**hey will then, **take** an **interest** in **your business**. They are your **future.**

Once again, do not forget that *Action* begets *Reaction*.

This will not happen overnight, because the lack of any display of ethical behavior on part of many in **Corporate America** in general has existed for too long.

I feel with every cell in my body, if you change your ways the rewards will be above and beyond belief for all Companies' stability and long term benefit.

My hope is that this will happen and this book will become antiquated to the point that there will no longer be a need for a book such as this.

Then and only then, will I be glad to say that now is the time that this book is ready to meet with the oval file.

Until there is no longer a need, the time for this book is **now**, and it is probably very much **overdue**.

Sharing some feelings:

Just because a Company's focus has produced a successful **bottom** line,

Doesn't necessarily prove, that it can be considered a **top** shelf Company.

If additionally, they show good ethical standards,

the conclusion, should be self **evident**.

Alan Mermelstein

CORPORATE AMERICA'S ETHICS CONTINUES DOWN THE

PORCELAIN CHAIR

[The End]

www.ingramcontent.com/pod-product-compliance
Lightning Source LLC
Chambersburg PA
CBHW022014170526
45157CB00003B/1242